WOODBURNING
PROJECTS AND PATTERNS FOR BEGINNERS

Bon Appétit

Minisa Robinson

FOX CHAPEL
PUBLISHING
www.FoxChapelPublishing.com

This book is dedicated to Jess, Will, Cash, and Alexis: you are my heart, my love, and my world.

Woodburning Projects and Patterns for Beginners is an original work, first published in 2020 by Fox Chapel Publishing Company, Inc. The patterns contained herein are copyrighted by the author. Readers may make copies of these patterns for personal use. The patterns themselves, however, are not to be duplicated for resale or distribution under any circumstances. Any such copying is a violation of copyright law.

ISBN 978-1-4971-0085-5

Library of Congress Control Number: 2020935270

To learn more about the other great books from Fox Chapel Publishing, or to find a retailer near you, call toll-free 800-457-9112 or visit us at *www.FoxChapelPublishing.com*.

We are always looking for talented authors. To submit an idea, please send a brief inquiry to acquisitions@foxchapelpublishing.com.

Printed in China
First printing

INTRODUCTION

Pyrography is an ancient art form where a hot tool is used to burn images onto wood, paper, gourds, leather, and other fire-friendly materials. It's more commonly known as woodburning because wood is often the medium of choice for the art form, and advancements in technology afford artists with various quality tools such as electric woodburning pens. Pyrography is incredibly versatile and can be used in countless ways, from adding simple embellishments onto carved wood, to decorating home décor items, and even creating high-quality realistic works of art.

This book is meant to teach the art of woodburning and ignite your artistic senses. Pyrography can be added to most species of unfinished wood, which opens a world of creative opportunities. The projects in this book also include the option for color, so the possibilities are endless.

A Timeline of Learning

This is a beginner's book, and before I show you my favorite artworks, I think it's important to show you my journey as a pyrographic artist. We all start as beginners and must grow from there. I am a self-taught artist, and most of my progress has come from a combination of trial, experiment, practice, and—above all else—attempting projects that were beyond my current skill level. Why? Because it was the catalyst that pushed me to greater learning. As artists, we are never stagnant, and we are always learning with each and every project. The willingness to learn is one of the greatest teachers in life, and I hope you will always be willing to attempt that next challenge. So, before we proceed, here are some of my first attempts at pyrography, which are also some of my most important projects.

This was the project that hooked me on pyrography. It was my first attempt at woodcarving with a Dremel® tool, and I was frustrated that I couldn't see my carving well. I purchased a simple woodburning tool from my local store and tried to burn over the carving so it would look better. I immediately learned a few things: first of all, woodcarving wasn't really my thing; secondly, I ruined my first woodburning point by pressing too hard; and lastly, I absolutely loved pyrography!

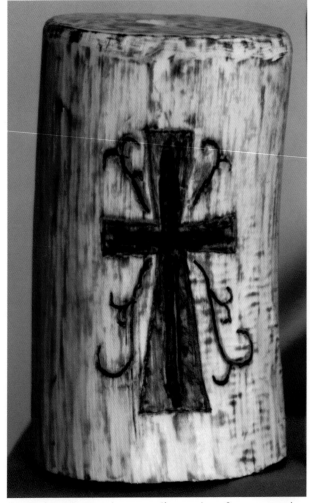
The project that made me realize my love for pyrography.

When I first started woodburning, I didn't have any wood to burn on, so I walked into the surrounding forests at my home in Colorado and cut down a small aspen tree with a hatchet. I peeled off the bark, cut it into small sections, and used that small tree for my first few pyrography projects.

I look back at my first project and know that I've learned so much since then, but that learning curve is so important to all artists. This was my first stepping-stone on my woodburning path.

Be willing to give life to new ideas.

My second woodburning project was on another small section of the aspen tree I cut down. At that time, I was afraid that the woodburning smoke would possibly trigger the smoke alarms of our small cabin, so I made this outside on the deck. It was a frigid autumn afternoon, and the woodburner was the only thing keeping my hands from getting too cold. I had no reference photo or guidelines and sketched out this small elk before dark. After the project was finished, I showed my husband, and his kind words were the spark that encouraged me to try again.

My second woodburning project, burned without any references.

Embrace the practice of practice.

This was my third project and the first time I used a printed-out reference photo with graphite paper. It was a big help to lay out the outlines of the piece, and I used the Dremel® tool to carve out the sun behind

the bison. At this point, I realized that my options for pyrography were truly unlimited and I couldn't wait to try more ideas.

Imagination and creativity know no bounds.

Most of my first projects were created on round pieces of aspen, but I wanted to try a flat piece, so my husband cut a slab of aspen with his chainsaw for me. This was my first flat woodburning, and I quickly realized the importance of sanding the wood before burning. The surface was very rough and difficult to burn on, and at this point, I was still experimenting with different tips and ways to use them. This woodburning piece was a huge learning experience, and it pushed me to create more realistic woodburnings.

My third project opened my eyes to the unlimited possibilities pyrography can offer.

My first flat project taught me the importance of first sanding your wood.

Never stop growing!

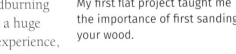

Chapter 1

WOODBURNING SAFETY AND SETUP

Woodburning is a delightful art form full of many possibilities. Because of its versatile nature, it's a good idea to learn more about the safety aspects of the art. Some woodburning tools can easily reach over 1,000 degrees F (540 degrees C); therefore, they present a possible danger of fire and personal burns. The following tips can help you enjoy the art of woodburning safely.

To reduce the risks of fire:
- Never leave a woodburner unattended.
- Keep combustible materials away from the hot tool.
- Keep pets and children away from the unit.
- Secure the hot burner with a stand or holder.
- Keep cords out from underfoot.
- Use common sense when handling the hot tool.

For personal safety:
- Burn in a well-ventilated area.
- Give yourself plenty of room to work.
- Wear a glove while burning to help protect your fingers.
- Never change out points with your hands; use needle-nosed pliers instead.
- Don't burn near water or liquids.
- Work on an incline to allow heat to rise up and away from your hand.
- An inclined surface can also help your back and neck.
- Never use a woodburning tool during an electrical storm.

To protect your lungs:
- Burn on unfinished wood only.
- Never burn over wood with a clear coat, varnish, paint, etc. Doing so could produce toxic fumes.
- Only add color after the burning is complete. Burning over pigments can also create toxic fumes.
- Never burn on plastic, medium-density fiberboard (MDF), particle boards, or any wood that is bound together with glues.
- Always wear a dust mask when sanding.
- Use a respirator for applying clear coats.
- If you burn on leather, choose vegetable-tanned leather only.
- Do your research before attempting to burn on a new wood species. Most woods are safe, but a few can produce toxins when burned. There are some resourceful websites on wood safety; however, if you're unsure, consult a wood specialist.

To protect the woodburner:
- Never change out points when a burner is on. You can damage the threads and/or shear the point off completely. Always wait until the woodburner has completely cooled before replacing points.
- Use light pressure when burning. Pressing down firmly can bend or damage the points or burner.

Keep the woodburning tool secure at all times.

Wearing a glove can protect against accidental burns. I use a simple gardening glove from my local store, but it has saved my fingers from excessive heat and unintentional burns.

Wear a respirator when applying clear coats or burning dark backgrounds, which can produce more smoke.

Bent point due to excessive pressure

Some artists plug in their burning unit and get comfy; burning in their easy chairs or even their beds. However, I strongly recommend working at a desk with adequate space and lighting. It's important to secure your woodburning tool while working to help prevent the risk of fire. Also, keep your workspace free of papers, tissues, or other flammable items. Finally, always keep beverages or water far from the electric burner!

A flat desk is a great start, but using an inclined desk can help prevent neck and back pain, making the woodburning experience more enjoyable. I purchased this adjustable drafting table from an online retailer, but you can also use a tabletop easel with some adjustment.

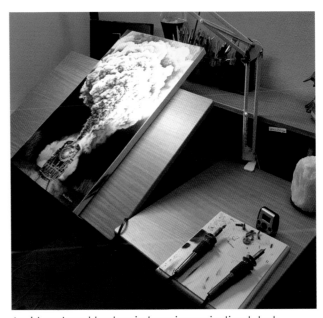

Avoid neck and back pain by using an inclined desk.

Chapter 2
TOOLS AND EQUIPMENT

It takes very few supplies to get started in pyrography, most of which are quite affordable. This makes it an appealing hobby or craft to people of all ages and backgrounds.

Woodburning Units

There are two main types of woodburners: soldering-iron type burners with interchangeable solid points, and units with interchangeable wire pens and nibs. There are many popular woodburners within each group, which allows artists to make their selection based on personal preference. People often ask me what is the "best" woodburning tool on the market, and I encourage them to find the one that best suits their style of burning. What works best for me may not work well for others, and likewise, other artists' preferences don't always work with my style. Sometimes it can take trial and error to see what works best for you.

Some artists convince themselves early in their learning curve that they could create better work if only they had better tools. While sometimes this can be the case, usually the quality of one's work comes from practice and learning the tools you have. The artist uses the tools; the tools don't make the artist. Great art is possible with simple tools.

I have both the Walnut Hollow® Creative Versa-Tool® and the Razertip® dual pen system, but I use the Versa-Tool for most of my work. Both units are very nice, but once again this comes down to my personal preference.

Walnut Hollow Creative Versa-Tool

This woodburning kit can be found at most craft stores and big-box retailers within the United States. It is a soldering-iron type burner and has a variable temperature control plus 11 interchangeable points. Once plugged in and turned on, the burner will reach optimal temperature in about five minutes but maintains a steady and consistent heat while burning.

Razertip SS-D10

This unit is found through online retailers and uses interchangeable wire tip pens and nibs. The pens are usually purchased separately since there are many to choose from, and they vary greatly based on the needs of the artist. The Razertip also comes with a variable temperature feature and reaches the optimal temperature almost instantly once turned on. This burner can also reach much higher temperatures to burn very hard woods or bone.

Woodburning Points: Walnut Hollow Overview

The Walnut Hollow Creative Versa-Tool comes with several different points, which can be very versatile. I've made a chart to help show the different burn styles that you can create with each point. These are only a few ideas, and I encourage you to experiment with each point to learn what works best for you.

Tip The brass points can be modified to suit your needs. They can be easily bent or can be sanded to create a smoother edge. If damaged, the points can be purchased individually from Walnut Hollow.

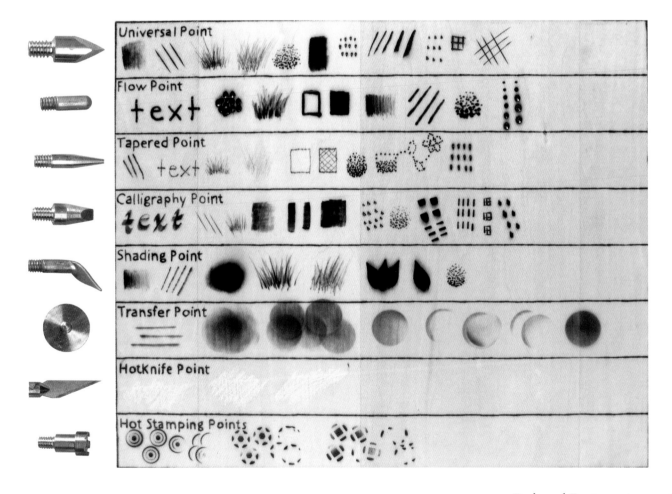

Versa-Tool: Universal Point

Side-Shading. Using the side of the bevel, drag the point sideways to create soft shading. (Sand the edge of the point if it's too sharp.)

Crisp Lines. Drag the sharp edge of the bevel downward to create crisp lines.

Grass. Turn the point upside down and use the upper edge of the point to drag upward in random strokes. This can create the illusion of grass.

Fur. Burn fur by drawing varied upward strokes. Then use side-shading to soften and blend them together.

Stippling/Pointillism. Use the upper point to create a unique stippling effect.

Solid Black. Very similar to side-shading, use the side of the bevel and drag very slowly in a horizontal motion.

Downward Triangles. Using the upper point, press into the wood to create a downward triangle.

Varied Lines. You can create lines of different thicknesses by tipping the universal point to the side and laying it flatter against the wood.

Upward Triangles. Using the lower point, press into the wood to create an upward triangle.

Boxes and Windows. Lightly press the front edge of the point into the wood to create each edge of a small box or window.

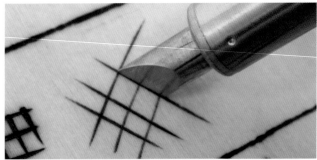

Crosshatching. Use the sharp edge of the point to create bold crosshatching.

Versa-Tool: Flow Point

Text. Burn text much like you'd use a pencil. Be sure to set the point down in a smooth motion, much like an airplane, to prevent those "stop spots."

Stippling. One of my favorite uses of this tip is to create unique textures through stippling. Press the point straight into the wood to make a circle-shaped indentation.

Grass and Fur. Use an upward stroke to create grass and fur textures. Because the point is larger, the grass or fur will have a softer and more blended feel.

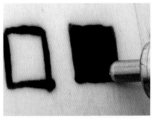

Borders and Solid Black. The flow point is great for burning dark outlines and for blocking in solid areas of black. I often use this technique for filling in larger text.

10 Woodburning Projects and Patterns for Beginners

Shading. You can use the flow point to create gradients and shading. Burn in a back-and-forth motion much like you'd draw with a pencil.

Lines. Use the flow point to make smooth and dark lines.

Stippling/Pointillism. The flow point is helpful when creating stippling or pointillism.

Circles. If you lightly touch the flow point to the wood, it will make a small circle or dot. The longer you press into the wood, the larger the dot will become. You can use this to create dots of different sizes.

Versa-Tool: Tapered Point

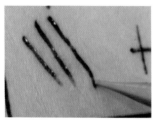

Fine Lines. Gently drag the point downward to create crisp, fine lines. Don't use hard pressure because this point can easily bend. (Yep, this was the first point I used and I bent it immediately.)

Text. The tapered point works great for drawing fine and intricate text.

Grass. Because this point is so small, it doesn't transfer a lot of heat to the wood. Therefore it can create some very fine and wispy grass.

Fur. Much like burning grass, this fine point can create light and delicate fur strokes.

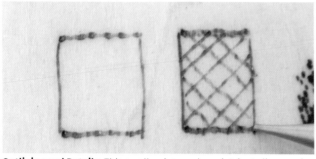

Outlining and Details. This small point can burn intricate lines and details by lightly dragging the point across the wood.

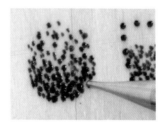

Stippling/Pointillism. While time consuming, this tapered point creates some very detailed stippling or pointillism. Although, because it's so tiny, I would recommend using this on smaller projects.

Inverted Teardrops. Lay the burner flat and gently press the point into the wood to create a tiny inverted teardrop shape.

Versa-Tool: Calligraphy Point

Text. As you might guess, the calligraphy point is designed for burning text in a calligraphic style.

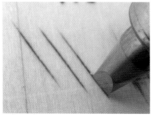

Crisp Lines. You can also create fine, crisp lines by burning with the edge of the sharp point.

Grass/Fur. Use the sharp edge of the point in upward strokes to create grass or fur.

Solid Black. Lay the burner flat and to the side, then slowly draw it to the side to block in dark areas.

Triangles. Press the upper point of the bevel into the wood to create small triangular shapes.

Stippling. You can create an unusual and unique stippling pattern with the upper point of the bevel.

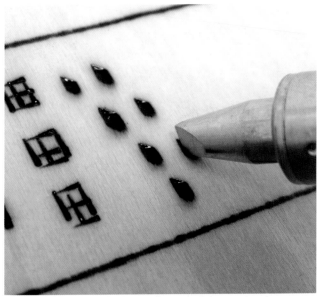

Diamond Shapes. Lay the burner flat toward the wood and gently press the upper point of the bevel down to create small diamond shapes.

Squares and Rectangles. Lay the burner flat toward the wood and use the upper flat edge of the bevel to create small square and rectangular shapes.

Consistent Lines. Gently press the flat edge of the point straight into the wood to create consistent, short lines.

Versa-Tool: Shading Point

Shading. Create gradients and soft shading by using the upper point of this versatile tip. Remember to set the point down gently, much like an airplane taking off and landing.

Lines. You can also use the upper point to draw fine lines. Don't use excessive downward pressure or you can bend the point.

Solid Black. Lay the point flat on the wood and slowly move the point back and forth to create a rich, solid black.

Grass. Roll the shading point to the side and use the edge in an upward motion to create blades of grass.

Fur. Create soft or crisp fur strokes by burning back-and-forth motions with the upper point of the shading tip.

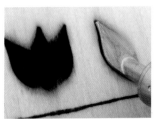

Leaf Shapes. Gently press the flat point onto the wood to create leaf shapes.

Stippling/Pointillism. Turn the point upside down and use the very tip to create tiny dots for stippling or pointillism.

Versa-Tool: Transfer Point

This point is designed to transfer an image onto the wood using an iron-on based paper. However, here are some other uses for the point.

Lines. This is an unusual way to use this point, but it produces an interesting effect. By using the side of the point and slowly rolling it forward like a tire, you can burn straight lines.

Shading. Place the point flat on the wood and slowly burn back-and-forth or in a circular motion to create soft shading.

Overlapping Circles. Press the point straight onto the wood and overlap the circles to create an interesting background or texture.

Partial Circles. To create a crescent shape, just burn with the outer edge of the point.

Versa-Tool: Hot Knife

This point is used mainly for cutting thin objects and doesn't transfer much heat. It will cut into the wood but doesn't leave a burn mark.

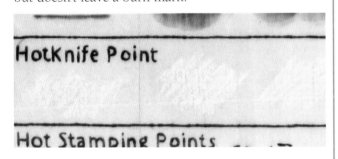

Versa-Tool: Stamping Points

Hot Stamps. These points each come with a unique shape that can be burned into the wood.

Woodburning Points: Razertip Overview

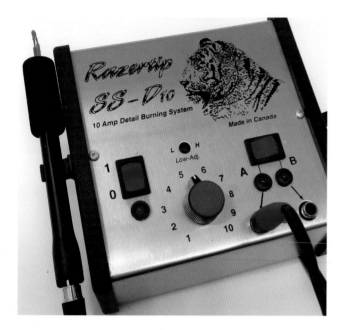

The Razertip woodburning tool comes as a base where you can purchase interchangeable pens separately. There is a huge variety of pens and nibs to choose from, and many of them are specialty-based for specific projects. Here are a few pens that are popular for general woodburning and work well for a wide range of subjects. These are some of my favorite pens, but I encourage you to experiment with these and other points to learn what works best for you.

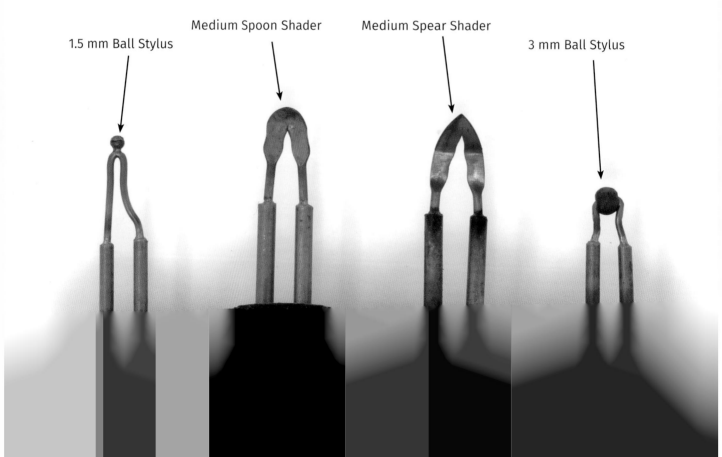

1.5 mm Ball Stylus

Medium Spoon Shader

Medium Spear Shader

3 mm Ball Stylus

Razertip: 1.5 mm Ball Stylus

Text. Use this small point to draw text, much like you'd use a pencil. Avoid excessive overburn markings by turning the heat dial to a lower setting.

Lines. You can easily draw in straight lines with this point, but again, use a lower temperature to create lines without overburn.

Stippling. This is a great point for fine stippling due to its smaller point size.

Varying Dots. You can create different-sized dots by placing the point on the wood for shorter or longer periods of time. Keep in mind that the longer the point is on the wood, the more likely you'll get overburn marks.

Razertip: 3 mm Ball Stylus

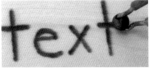

The 3 mm Ball Stylus can do everything that the smaller 1.5 mm Ball Stylus does, but it's a bit bigger and is well suited to larger projects. It is also great for blocking in areas as shown above.

Razertip: Medium Spear Shader

Fine Lines and Crosshatching. Turn the pen over and use the sharp edge of the point to create fine lines and crosshatching.

Angles. Lightly press the upper part of the point against the wood to create small angled shapes.

Solid Black. Lay the point flat on the wood and slowly move the point back and forth to create a rich, solid black.

Shading. This is a great point for creating soft shading. Just keep the point level at all times, because you can create an accidental hard line if you rock the point too much to one side or the other.

Razertip: Medium Spoon Shader

 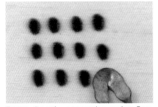  
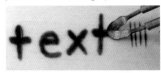

Fur. Create soft or crisp fur strokes by burning back-and-forth motions with the upper point of the shading tip.

Dots. Gently press the point flat into the wood to create uniform oval-shaped dots.

Text. You can also use this point to create text with soft edges, as well as sharp lines and crosshatching.

Shading. This is also a great point for creating soft shading. You don't need to keep the point flat all the time; it's okay to rock back and forth without creating harsh edge lines.

Solid Black. Lay the point flat on the wood and slowly move the point back and forth to create a rich, solid black.

Helpful Accessories

1. **Needle-nosed pliers.** For installing and removing interchangeable points.

2. **Tape measure.** Used to measure the wood dimensions for the design and layout.

3. **Clear tape.** To affix a reference photo onto the wood while transferring with graphite paper.

4. **Sandpaper 220–600 grit.** To sand the wood before burning.

5. **Scissors.** For cutting out the reference photo.

6. **Knife blade.** For scraping or removing woodburning mistakes.

7. **Red ballpoint pen.** When transferring an image with graphite paper, a red pen often shows up better than a black pen.

8. **Graphite paper.** To transfer a design or image onto the wood.

9. **Timer.** To keep track of hours on a project if you bill by the hour.

10. **Glove.** To help protect your hand from accidental burns.

11. **Respirators.** To protect your lungs when applying clear coats, finishes, stains, etc.

12. **Dust mask.** Always wear a dust mask when sanding.

13. **Soft pad or beanbag.** To help support your wrist while burning.

Chapter 3

WOOD TYPES

There are many different types of wood that can be burned on safely. I'll be covering some of the more common and easily accessible wood species in this chapter. Remember that even a safe type of wood becomes dangerous to burn once it has been clear-coated, painted, treated, etc. Always burn on unfinished wood only. If you're unsure whether or not you can burn on a particular species of wood, please contact a forestry specialist.

Basswood

Basswood is one of the most popular woods to burn on and is certainly my personal preference. It can be a little more expensive that other common wood types, but it can make a huge difference in your quality of work. Basswood is also known as linden and is found in eastern North America. It has a very light color, with minimal grain and growth rings, which makes it especially nice to burn on. Since it is a popular wood for woodburning artists and carvers alike, basswood comes in a variety of different sizes, styles, and cuts.

The lighter color of basswood makes it great for a wide range of tones, from jet blacks to blonde highlights.

BASSWOOD

Other popular surfaces for pyrography include:
- Maple
- Italian poplar
- Watercolor paper
- Gourds
- Leather

Birch

Birch is quite light, and it has an overall uniform appearance with minimal grain. It's often sold in panels of a variety of thicknesses that are glued to thicker panels for support. If you choose to burn on birch panels, be sure you don't burn deeply into the lower layers of glue. (As a personal rule, I never burn solid black backgrounds on any plywood-based wood to avoid releasing potentially toxic fumes.)

Pine

Pine is usually inexpensive and easy to find at most craft stores and lumberyards. However, it can be challenging to burn on. The heavy grain can cause your point to zig and zag, which makes it difficult to burn straight lines. Some artists have good luck burning on "kiln-dried" pine, but most pieces of pine that are readily available haven't gone through this process. Therefore, pine contains a lot of pitch and creates a lot of smoke when burned on.

If you choose to burn on pine, I recommend using a respirator suited for particulates or work in a well-ventilated area.

Cherry

Cherry is a beautiful wood that is quite soft. Even though the grain is very visible, the lines don't interfere with the point of the burner. This wood burns on the darker side very easily, and lighter shading produces a slightly reddish tint.

Because cherry is darker than other woods, adding paint or colored pencils after burning can produce amazingly vivid results.

Butternut

Much like cherry, butternut is also a darker wood and is quite soft. I find that it is well suited to darker subjects and it combines nicely with paint or colored pencils. These butternut slices are quite large, with some interesting knots and irregularities. I purchased these from a private supplier, but you can find them online from specialty lumberyards.

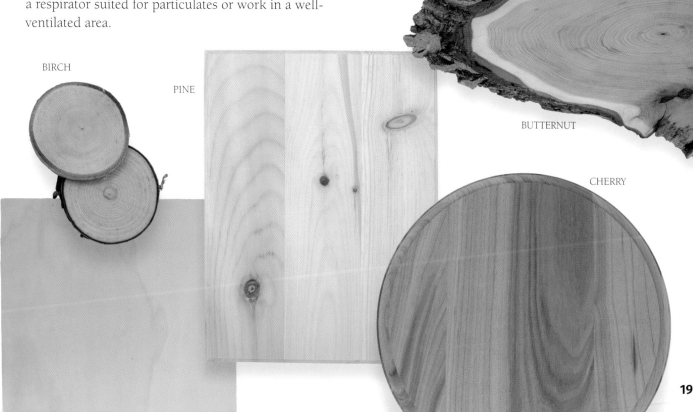

BIRCH

PINE

BUTTERNUT

CHERRY

Chapter 4

BEFORE YOU BURN

Pyrography is a very exciting art form, but before we dive right into burning, there are a few more things to go over first.

When selecting a piece of wood for pyrography, it's important to use one that is free of large cracks since the wood can expand with heat. If those cracks expand too much, they can even split the wood apart. If you're working on a specific project, such as a portrait, you might choose wood without knots or blemishes.

Avoid touching the front of the wood with your fingers. Fingers and hands contain natural oils that can be deposited onto the wood. These oils can show up after burning your image. Also, avoid handling your wood after applying lotions to your hands. Get into the habit of washing your hands before burning to help remove any substances that might stain or damage the wood.

Prepare the Wood

Most wood comes planed and ready to use, however it helps to sand the wood prior to woodburning. This makes an even surface and helps reduce the buildup of carbon on the woodburning points. Always wear a dust mask when sanding.

Start by sanding the front of the wood with a rough-grit sandpaper and work toward 220-grit sandpaper, then finish it off by using 330 grit. This is adequate for most purposes, but if you'd like an extra smooth surface, you can sand with 400 grit or more. I usually sand to 600 grit, but I know of other artists that sand up to 800 or 1200 grit; additional sanding is more of a personal preference. As a note, I don't sand the backside of the wood.

After sanding, use a soft cloth to wipe down the surface of the wood.

You can even use canned air to remove the sawdust from rustic bark edges. When you're finished sanding, carefully gather up the sawdust and clean your workspace.

How to Use Patterns

The patterns included in this book are a great tool to get started woodburning. Here are some tips on how to utilize them.

Tip You don't need to be a computer guru! There are many online tips and tutorials for resizing images, or you can ask a computer-savvy friend to assist you. You can even make copies at your local library.

1

Start by creating a digital copy of the pattern. You can simply take a photo of the pattern and upload it onto a computer, use a scanner, or take the pattern to a local copy store.

2

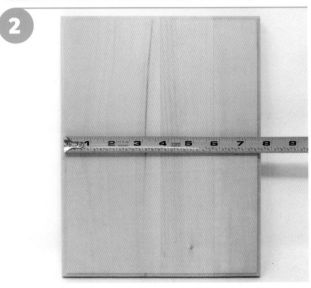

Measure the length and width dimensions of your wood.

3

Adjust the size of the digital pattern to fit the physical dimensions of your piece of wood.

4

Print out the pattern.

5

Use scissors or a paper cutter to trim the pattern to fit the wood.

6

After the pattern has been trimmed, tape it to the wood on two sides.

Tip Since I am right-handed, I prefer to tape the pattern at the top and right sides. This helps keep the graphite paper out from under my working hand. Also, it's helpful to tape two sides down onto your workspace so the pattern doesn't shift accidentally while working.

7

After taping the pattern to the wood, lift it and gently slide the graphite paper between the wood and pattern. (Be sure that the graphite side is down.)

8

Transfer the pattern onto the wood by using a red pen to draw overtop of the guidelines. Use a firm pressure, but don't press so hard that you dent the wood underneath. (The red pen shows up a little better than a black one, which makes it easier to see which lines you may have missed.)

9

When drawing over the guidelines, it can be reassuring to peek underneath the graphite paper occasionally to ensure that the pattern is transferring appropriately. (I can tell you from personal experience that it can be devastating to spend an hour transferring a pattern, only to realize that the graphite paper was upside down.)

10

After transferring the pattern, take a moment and make sure the entire pattern is present. Then remove the graphite paper and pattern from the wood. If the guidelines seem too dark, you can sand them lightly with a fine-grit sandpaper. (Keep in mind that if you burn overtop of the graphite paper guidelines, it can be more difficult to remove them later. Therefore, I prefer to sand the guidelines prior to burning.) Once you're happy with the transfer, start burning and have fun!

Create Your Own Design

Patterns are wonderful and take a lot of the guesswork out of woodburning. However, if you'd like to try your own ideas and designs, here are a few tips.

How to Choose a Strong Design

When selecting a design for woodburning, I often spend countless hours scouring over reference photos before finally settling on an image.

Here are some points I consider when choosing a new subject for my pyrographic artwork:

1. **Personal interest.** Burn images that you enjoy. Artists will often create better work when they are passionate about their subject. Remember, art is supposed to be fun!
2. **Quality references.** I generally work from photographs and can speak from experience that a reference photo with poor quality will produce an artwork of poor quality. The higher the resolution, the better your woodburning will turn out, especially when burning large pieces.
3. **Composition.** Spend a lot of time searching for the right composition and design. In my opinion, it can make or break a piece. It shouldn't be confusing or distracting. There should be no question as to what you're looking at; therefore, there's no guessing on the part of the viewer.
4. **Remove the distractions.** If there are confusing parts, do your best to remove them using artistic license. Removing branches or grass in front of the subject will make it stand out in a more crisp and clean manner. You can also add elements at your own discretion, but don't allow minor elements to hide the most important features of your composition.
5. **Light source.** I prefer a strong sense of light in my work. It creates more depth and realism, and brings more life to the subject. It is also more visually striking.
6. **The pose of the subject.** When creating a woodburning of a person or animal, take careful note of how the subject is posing. Is the subject standing in a funny pose that makes him or her look distorted? Can you see all the important features of the subject or are some of them hidden?
7. **Cropping.** Cropping is a great way to draw your eyes to the key elements of an artwork. Have you cropped out too much of the subject, or do you have too much dead space and need to crop out the extra fluff? Avoid splitting your composition directly in half. This is especially important with landscapes. If you're burning a mountain scene with a river, for instance, you need to decide which part of the painting should have the most focus. If the mountains are more important, make sure they take up more than half of your composition.
8. **Size.** When composing an image with several subjects, decide which one is the most important and make sure that it takes up the largest area of your "canvas."

Where to Find Reference Photos

As an artist that specializes in realistic art, I find that working from high-quality reference photos is critical. Inspiration can be found all around us, especially in our digital world with access to millions of photos. However, be aware that you can easily violate copyright laws by making a woodburning from a copyrighted photograph. The safest way to avoid copyright infringement is to ask permission from the original photographer to create an artwork based on the photo. If that's not possible, there are some fantastic websites and Facebook groups dedicated to offering reference photos; just search for "reference photos for artists."

As always, please read the fine print on each resource, as their policies may change over time.

Disclaimer: For copyright questions and laws, please contact a copyright lawyer.

Startup Time

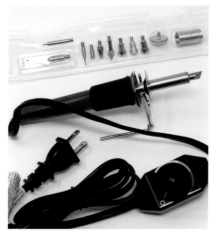

When using a soldering iron type of burner, such as the Walnut Hollow Creative Versa-Tool, allow it to warm up for about five minutes before working. Always be sure that the burner is secure and don't leave it unattended while warming up.

A burning unit with nibs or pens usually heats up immediately and doesn't require a wait time.

Tip

Always use pliers to change out solid points. **Note:** Never change out points when the burner is hot! You can damage the threads or break the points and burner. Always wait until completely cool before switching out points.

Tips for Holding the Burner

Hold the woodburning unit by grasping the rubber grip with your fingertips, much like you would hold a pencil. Some burners have a foam or cork grip. Never attempt to hold or touch the metal parts.

Your grip should be firm but comfortable when burning. If you squeeze the grip too tightly, your hand can become fatigued. I also find that the larger grips are more comfortable when working. Like any new skill, allow your hand to adjust to woodburning and give it small breaks while you work.

You might want to support your wrist while woodburning to avoid any fatigue or discomfort in the wrist. This is especially helpful when using woodburning units such as the Walnut Hollow Creative Versa-Tool since the grip is a couple inches (centimeters) away from the tip. The closer the grip is to the point, the less you'll need to support your wrist.

Note: I prefer to wear a glove while woodburning, but this isn't required. I use a simple gardening glove that I purchased from my local store many years ago. It helps a little to reduce the heat on my hand, but not much. The main reason I wear this is to help prevent accidental burns.

Shorter Grip

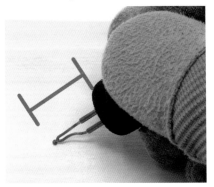

If the grip is located close to the point, then you can rest your hand on the wood and burn comfortably without a wrist support.

> **Tip** Your hand will get hotter if you're working on a flat surface. Try switching to an incline instead. It allows the heat to rise away from your hand instead of accumulating directly underneath.
>
>
>
> I use an art table that has an adjustable top. You can also use a small tabletop easel or just prop up your work using books.

Longer Grip

Some woodburning units have the grip built much farther from the point.

Supported Wrist

Unsupported Wrist

An unsupported wrist with a grip positioned far from the point can make it difficult to rest the wrist on the wood without creating a bend in the joint.

You can use a soft, bean-filled bag or a rolled-up sock to prop up and align the wrist to help avoid fatigue or pain. This gives you more control and steadiness when burning. You can even use your other hand or arm to help support your wrist.

> **Tip** If you're burning on a piece of wood with a heavy grain, then it can make it difficult to burn a straight line. When holding the burner straight up
>
>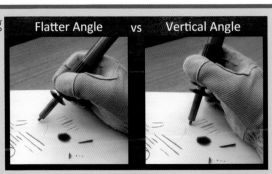
>
> Flatter Angle   vs   Vertical Angle
>
> and down, the point wants to sink down into the wood fibers, and these rings or lines can make the point jump to the side. Holding the burner at a flatter angle can help.

Chapter 5

TEMPERATURE BASICS

Most woodburning tools come with an adjustable temperature dial. This allows the user to easily increase or decrease the temperature of the woodburning point. When using a soldering-iron type of burner, remember to allow a few minutes for the burner to adjust for temperature changes. Pen-type burners usually adjust their temperature very quickly.

If your burner does NOT have an adjustable setting, there are a few ways to cool the point manually. You can set up a fan to continually blow air onto the point, or you can lightly blow on the point with your breath. (This is something I do often, even while using an adjustable burner. It's a quick and easy way to lower the temperature while working.)

You can also control the darkness of your lines by practicing your stroke speed. The faster you move a point across the wood, the lighter the line will be. By contrast, your lines will be darker if you move the point very slowly.

It's easy to learn the different temperature settings of a burner by creating a simple "temperature

Many burners have temperature control dials. This makes burning lighter tones much easier. This is a simple example of the temperature zones for the Walnut Hollow Creative Versa-Tool.

swatch" such as the one above. (Just be sure to allow the burner a few minutes to adjust into each temperature range.) Also, be aware that different types of wood will produce slightly different shades and values, so have fun and create multiple temperature swatches.

Temperature Chart

A temperature chart is designed to help you learn the different dial settings for the Razertip woodburning unit. Creating a chart like this is a great way to practice heat settings and learn how the pens handle the increasing temperatures. Usually the thinner points will burn more easily with a lower setting, and the thicker points operate better at higher settings. (See page 128 for the chart pattern.)

To create your own chart, copy the pattern on page 128 and print it out on a piece of paper. Tape it to the appropriately sized piece of wood and use graphite paper to transfer the main guidelines. (On page 28, I left the guidelines unburned in order to see the subtle changes in gradation. However, feel free to burn over those guidelines if it helps to see the different temperature zones.)

Begin by setting your burner to level 1, wait for a few moments, then see what marks you can make in the doodle zone. Don't worry if you don't see a mark right away; try leaving the point on the wood for a few seconds to see if the point will transfer any heat. If you still don't see anything, set the burner to level 2, wait a few moments, and repeat the process. (Some tips won't transfer enough heat on the lower settings to burn a mark onto the wood, but starting at level 1 and working your way up through the different temperature settings is a great way to learn about each point.)

After trying different points in the doodle zone for each temperature setting, return the dial back to level 1 and begin burning the stippling, lines, shading, and gradients for each level on the dial. Remember to give the points a moment or two to adjust to any new temperature setting for a more accurate result. Be mindful of how long the point touches the wood and use that to your advantage: use slower strokes with a lower temperature and faster strokes with the higher temperatures to moderate the difference in heat.

These points and techniques are just a suggestion, so feel free to mix things up and create your own chart if you'd like; the learning curve is part of the fun! The chart on page 28 was burned onto basswood, so try different types of wood as well.

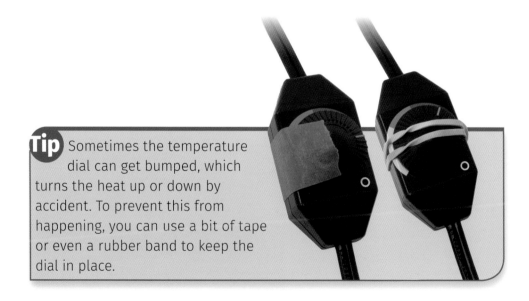

Tip Sometimes the temperature dial can get bumped, which turns the heat up or down by accident. To prevent this from happening, you can use a bit of tape or even a rubber band to keep the dial in place.

This temperature chart is designed to learn the different dial settings for the Razertip woodburning unit.

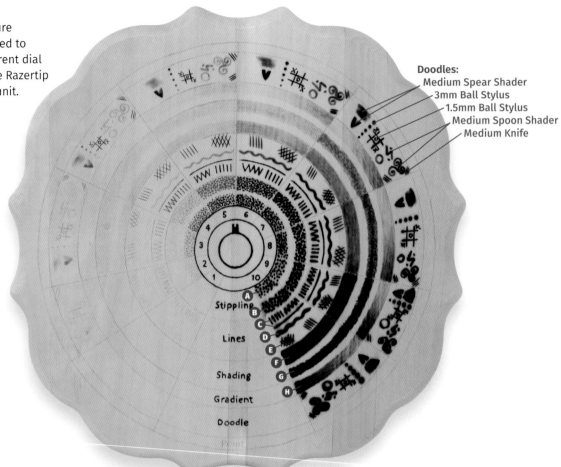

Doodles:
- Medium Spear Shader
- 3mm Ball Stylus
- 1.5mm Ball Stylus
- Medium Spoon Shader
- Medium Knife

Stippling
Lines
Shading
Gradient
Doodle

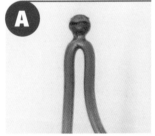

A Stippling created with the 1.5mm (¹⁄₁₆") Ball Stylus

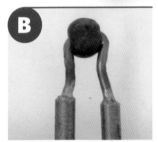

B Stippling created with the 3mm (¹⁄₈") Ball Stylus

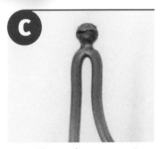

C Short lines, zig zags, and a long line created with the 1.5mm (¹⁄₁₆") Ball Stylus

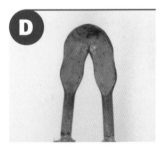

D Wavy line created with the Medium Spoon Shader

E Crosshatching and lines created with the Medium Knife

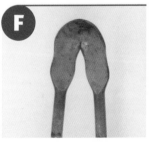

F Solid shading created with the Medium Spoon Shader

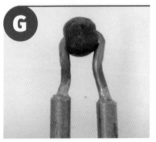

G Circle shading created with the 3mm (¹⁄₈") Ball Stylus

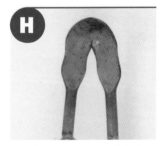

H Gradients created with the Medium Spoon Shader

Chapter 6
SHADING BASICS

Shading is a range of tones that makes an object look three-dimensional.

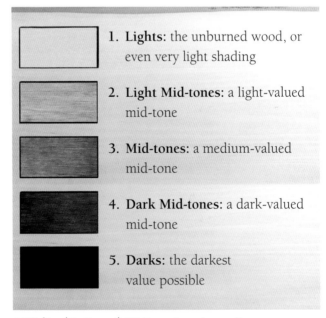

It's a great way to provide depth in an image by visually pushing and pulling different areas to and from the viewer. Dark areas tend to push away from the viewer, while lighter areas usually pull toward the viewer. A great example of this is Egyptian hieroglyphs or other carvings. As you can see, the darkest areas appear deeper or farther away, and the lightest areas are raised and appear closer. This ability to push and pull is a great way to create the illusion of depth in your artwork.

Three-Step Shading

Shading in pyrography doesn't need to be complicated. The first and most important step to shading is to begin training your eyes to see the different basic values. Take what you see and break it down into lights, mid-tones, and darks (as listed below), then blend these values together for a smoother appearance. (Keep in mind that shading values can vary slightly depending on the type of wood used.)

1. **Lights:** the unburned wood, or even very light shading

2. **Mid-tones:** a medium-valued mid-tone

3. **Darks:** the darkest value possible

Five-Step Shading

You can also take that basic, three-step shading scale to the next level and work with a five-step system. This is the shading scale that I prefer to work with and use it most for my instructional materials. (White is

also added to this scale as Level 0, by adding colored pencils or paint. This is a personal decision of the artist and completely optional.)

Keep in mind that this scale was created on basswood and different types of wood will produce slightly different shades. Feel free to experiment and create a shading scale like the one below on multiple types of wood.

1. **Lights:** the unburned wood, or even very light shading

2. **Light Mid-tones:** a light-valued mid-tone

3. **Mid-tones:** a medium-valued mid-tone

4. **Dark Mid-tones:** a dark-valued mid-tone

5. **Darks:** the darkest value possible

0 White: (Optional) White colored pencils or paint can be added.

Shading by the Numbers

As you begin to train your eyes to see the different values, you can use the shading scales to create different moods within a project. (The pattern for this toilet paper roll is available on page 130.)

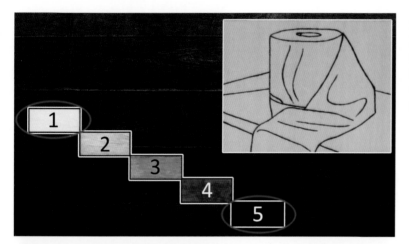

Example 1: This simple image uses only Level 1 and Level 5. It's basically a black and white line drawing. This example has no real shading to speak of. By leaving out the mid-tones, the image looks very simple and flat, with no depth.

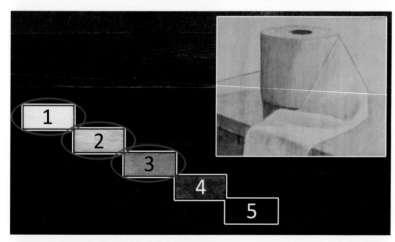

Example 2: The sample here shows an image created with the lightest shading tones. It's something that's very common with beginning artists who may be unsure of how dark to burn. This image has a lot more depth than the simple black and white version; however, it's still quite light and we are missing out on some of those rich, darker tones.

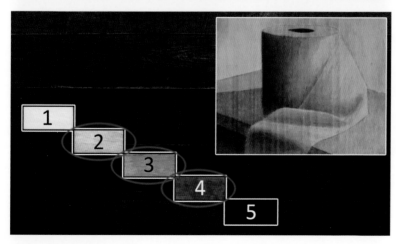

Example 3: This example shows a burning using only the mid-tones. Once again, this has more depth than the previous image, but by leaving out the lightest highlights and the darkest shadows, we don't see much definition or contrast in the image.

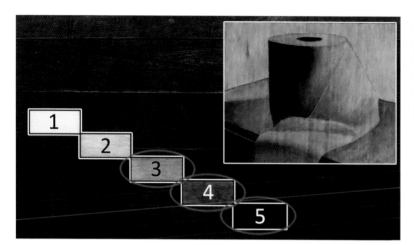

Example 4: Here is an image that is burned with the darkest values on the scale. It has a lot of rich, deep tones, but overall it looks a bit too dark. By leaving out the lightest tones, we are missing out on those subtle and smooth highlights.

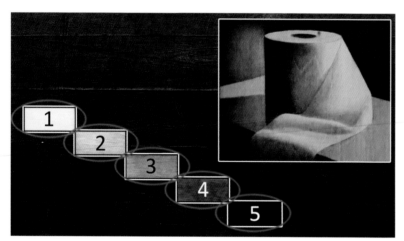

Example 5: Finally, we have an image that incorporates all of the levels on the shading scale. The whitest highlights paired with the dark black creates a vivid contrast, while the mid-tones offer a rich variety of depth.

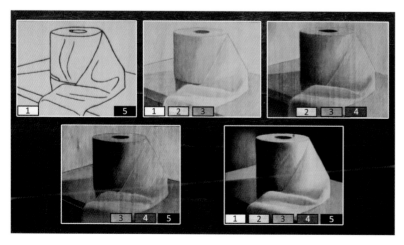

Review: By creating different shading versions of the same image, it helps to train your eyes to see the different values within a piece. These examples are also a great way to create different moods within a project. If you want a softer, more delicate feeling, then stay on the lighter range of the scale. If you're looking for a dark and somber mood, then use the lower end of the shading scale. Personally, I prefer dramatic contrast in my artwork, so I tend to use the entire shading scale. Oftentimes, I'll add white colored pencil after the burn for an extra level of depth, but this is a personal preference.

Chapter 7

PRACTICE THE FUNDAMENTALS

When woodburning, it's important to develop a strong foundation of basic skills. Every image that is created with pyrography can be broken down to a few basic fundamentals. These include learning how to create basic lines/strokes, changing directions with the burner, creating curves and circles, shading, and gradients. As you begin to woodburn, practice these fundamentals so that they become natural and fluid movements.

Tip It's helpful to keep a scrap piece of wood nearby while woodburning. This allows you to test your current temperature settings before using the burner on a project. Sometimes your burner might be turned up too high and it burns a dark spot immediately upon contact with the wood, which can be very frustrating. Instead, create a quick test burn on your scrap wood to dial in the temperature. You can also use that scrap wood to experiment with different points or techniques before using them on your project.

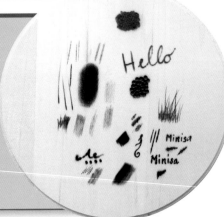

Tip Be careful not to burn too hot, too fast. While it's tempting to turn the temperature dial to maximum, this can easily damage the surface of the wood, especially when using pen and nib burners such as the Razertip. Burning too hot will also produce "overburn" and can create excessive carbon buildup on the points.
  Also, if your burner is digging into the wood, much like a farmer's plow, then you're using too much heat or pressing too hard.

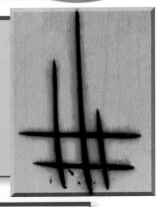

Tip Always use light pressure when woodburning. Most wood will compress or dent somewhat when you burn across it; however, if you press down really hard when burning, you can bend or break the point and/or burner. "Float" the point across the surface of the wood lightly, moving slowly and burning with heat instead of pressure.

Practice: Basic Lines

Burning consistent and even lines is a fundamental skill of woodburning. Here are some simple exercises to practice the basics of line control. Remember that repetition is the key to mastering a new skill, so grab a slab of wood and fill it with these practice strokes. (Feel free to substitute the points shown if needed or try these practice exercises with multiple points.)

Avoid the "Stop Spot"

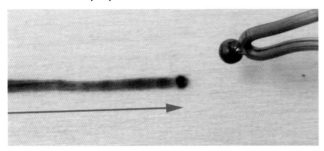

As beginners, we often make this simple mistake when woodburning:
1. Set the point on the wood.
2. Burn the line and stop.
3. Lift the point off the wood.

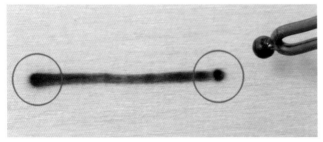

However, these three steps often produce a "stop spot" on both ends of the line. These spots are a result of leaving the point on the wood too long and can appear unsightly.

Use Gentle Transitions

To help avoid the stop spot, try placing the point of the burner onto the wood gently and gradually, much like an airplane would land smoothly onto a runway. Then once your line is complete, lift the point off the wood in the same smooth motion, like an airplane gently taking off. Practice this transition until it becomes habit so that each time the point touches down or leaves the wood, it is done so gradually.

Tip Burn with heat instead of pressure. Try to use a light pressure and not dig the point into the wood while burning. This can damage the wood and possibly bend the point.

Basic Stroke

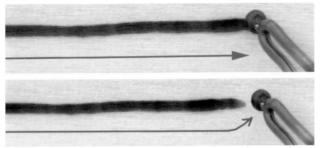

Set your burner to a medium heat and begin by burning a simple line with the grain of the wood. Try to use the gentle transition on and off of the wood with each stroke to minimize the stop spots. Use a light pressure and allow the point to float across the wood while it burns.

Slow Stroke

Fast Stroke

As you become familiar with burning the basic stroke, try burning it slowly and then quickly. (Don't adjust your temperature setting.) The burner will transfer more heat when it's moved slowly, and this will produce a darker line. If the point is moved across the wood quickly, it doesn't transfer much heat and will result in a lighter line.

Stroke speed can play a big part in controlling the darkness of a line without manually adjusting the temperature of the woodburner.

Tip Downward pressure will create an uneven line when burning against the grain.

Cross-Grain Strokes

Next, turn the wood and burn the regular strokes against the wood grain. You'll notice that the pen wants to sink down in between the grain and

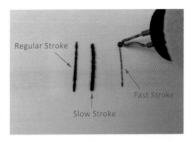

rise up again. This makes it more challenging to burn even lines against the wood grain. Try burning slower strokes and quicker strokes to learn how the pen reacts to the cross-grain.

Diagonal Strokes

Repeat the basic, slow, and fast strokes on a diagonal angle across the wood grain.

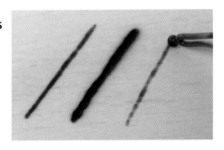

Push Away . . .

. . . and Pull Toward You

Try burning a basic stroke by pushing the pen upward and away from you. Then reverse the stroke and pull it down toward you. A lot of artists find that it's easier to pull the pen downward when making lines, but feel free to become familiar with each option. Try the push-and-pull strokes with the grain, then turn the wood and go across the grain as well.

Single Long Stroke

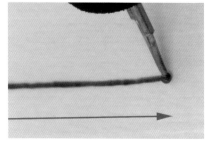

When burning a long line, you may choose to burn it in a single and continuous stroke. Practice making the long line as smooth and even as possible. You may notice that the line will get lighter toward the end as the heat is pulled out of the point.

Several Short Strokes

You can also burn long lines by creating a series of shorter strokes and blending them together. These shorter strokes will maintain the heat better in the pen and produce a more consistently dark line.

Practice: Changing Direction

As you become comfortable burning straight lines, it's time to practice changing direction with the burner.

Avoid the Stop Spot

It's easy to get a stop spot every time you change direction with the woodburner, especially if you pause when turning. See page 33 for instructions on how to avoid this issue.

Separate Strokes

Start practicing by creating two separate strokes and joining them together. Do your best to merge the strokes seamlessly without gaps or overlaps. This helps you to get a feel for where the point should be when you set it down on the wood.

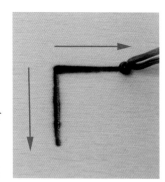

Single Stroke

Try changing direction smoothly in one stroke without lifting the burner. If you move the point faster in the corner, it can help avoid the stop spot.

Multiple Directions

Lastly, spend some time creating shapes or doodles with multiple directional changes. Try to make them as smooth and even as possible without spots. You may find that you need to turn the temperature down on the burner to help control the changes in direction, or you can utilize stroke speed techniques instead.

Practice: Curves and Circles

After burning straight lines and changing directions, you can practice making curved lines and circles on the wood.

Counterclockwise

Practice making curved strokes by pulling them toward you in a counterclockwise rotation. Set the point onto the wood in a smooth transition to help avoid the stop spot.

Clockwise

Create curved strokes by pushing them away from you in a clockwise rotation. Try to make these curved lines as smooth and as even as possible. Feel free to burn the curved strokes faster and slower, or even adjust the temperature to see what works best for you.

Single Long Stroke

Practice burning circles in a single, smooth stroke (either clockwise or counterclockwise). See if you can create a circle without that pesky stop spot.

Several Short Strokes

Next, try burning circles using several shorter strokes and blend them together to create a seamless stroke.

Practice: Shading

Shading is a great way to add depth and realism to your woodburnings. There are many different ways to shade when woodburning, so try them all to see what suits you best. Some methods are great for smaller areas, while others work well with larger projects. Here are some basic strokes to practice, but feel free to experiment with different methods as well.

Back-and-Forth Strokes

My favorite method of shading is to use a simple back-and forth-motion. Make sure that each stroke is performed with a gentle transition both onto the wood and when lifting off the wood. (In this picture, I'm showing the individual strokes separated so they can be seen more easily, but try to keep the strokes tight and together when shading.)

Back-and-Forth Strokes (Blend)

Try burning the back-and-forth strokes very close together to create a smooth shaded area. You can burn several layers to blend the strokes together.

Downward Strokes

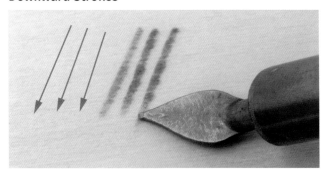

Another way to shade an area is to use consistent, downward strokes. (Once again, the strokes are separated in this example, but keep the strokes together when shading.)

Downward Strokes (Blend)

Try shading a section using the downward strokes, keeping them close together and blending them with multiple layers.

Crosshatching Strokes

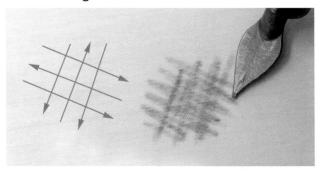

Some artists like to use a crosshatching stroke for shading. In this example, I'm using a back-and-forth stroke as mentioned earlier, then turning the wood and repeating the back-and-forth stroke at a 90-degree angle.

Cross Strokes (Blend)

After practicing this method, try shading in an area, making the strokes as smooth and blended as possible.

Keys to Smooth Shading:
- Gentle transitions on and off the wood
- Use a light touch
- Burn multiple layers
- Blend, blend, blend

Tips for Shading Larger Areas

Avoid Shading in Blocks

When shading large areas, it can be tempting to burn in systematic sections similar to the example to the right. However, this can create an unusual burn pattern with darker lines in between where the sections have overlapped.

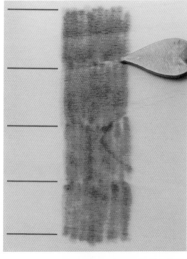

Instead of "marching" the burner across the wood in rows, try burning smooth sections with irregular edges.

These edges can be easier to blend together for a seamless appearance.

Circle Shading – One Layer

Circle shading can be a fun alternative to using lines. Gently place the burner on the wood and begin drawing small, connected circles. At first, you'll easily see the distinct lines, but keep going. The faster you move the burner, the lighter the shading will be, and vice versa.

Circle Shading – Multiple Layers

Burn multiple layers of circle shading to produce a more even value. This is a great way to create texture while you shade.

Circle Shading – Blending

You can also create gradients by blending the darker values into the lighter ones. This method of circle shading can be useful when burning larger areas; however, it can be more difficult to use in small, tight areas.

One Layer

Regardless of which method of shading you choose, it's helpful to burn multiple layers. In the picture to the right, there's only one layer of shading and bits of unburned wood can be seen in between the strokes. This can happen if the strokes aren't close enough to one another.

Multiple Layers

If you burn multiple layers, it's easier to achieve more complete coverage of the wood. Multiple layers are also helpful to blend the strokes for smoother shading.

Shading Swatches

As you become more comfortable with shading smooth areas, take some time and practice burning the different values of the shading scale. Try burning small shaded sections, then burn larger ones.

Level 2: Light Mid-tones

Level 3: Mid-tones

Level 4: Dark Mid-tones

Level 5: Darks

Practice: Solid Black/Black Backgrounds

I love burning black backgrounds! They can create vivid contrast between the subject and background, or they can envelop a subject in a shroud of mystery. Over the years, I've tried many different tools, temperatures, techniques, and wood types; however, I prefer to use the shading point of the Walnut Hollow Creative Versa-Tool burner for my black backgrounds.

Sanding Is Crucial

Sanding the wood is an important step to creating solid, black backgrounds. Without sanding, it's difficult for the burner to penetrate to the lower areas of an uneven surface. This creates light streaks in your background.

Avoid Excessive Heat

Another important step to burning a solid, dark black background is patience. If you burn too hot and too fast, then your background will be patchy, with some areas of scorched wood and others that are too light.

Higher temperature burners, such as the Razertip, are great for burning on hard surfaces such as bone, but the maximum temperature can be too much for most types of wood. It can easily damage the top layers of wood, which causes them to peel away and reveal the lighter layers underneath.

If you use a soldering iron, like the Walnut Hollow Creative Versa-Tool, the maximum heat setting usually works well for burning black backgrounds.

Wood Type Is Important

Wood type can play an important role in achieving a solid black. My favorite wood is basswood because it has minimal grain and no pitch or sap. Pine can be more difficult to burn because of the veins of sap.

> **Tip** Thinner points don't hold the heat as well as thicker points; therefore, it's helpful to use a larger point for burning a consistent black.

Go with the Grain

Burning with the grain produces a smoother black than burning across the grain. This is especially noticeable with larger burns because the point tends to sink down in between the grains of the wood when burning cross-grain.

Lay the shading point flat on the wood and slowly burn back and forth in small sections.

Burn in Small Sections

It also helps to burn small sections very slowly and develop a deep black before moving on. Working in smaller areas allows the heat to penetrate deep into the wood and creates a more consistent black. If you burn across larger sections at a time, the wood pulls the heat out of the burner and results in a lighter value.

Be sure to blend each section together so there are no gaps or light areas.

Continue burning across the wood in small sections to create a dark, solid black.

One of the coolest aspects of a solid black background is the reflection. The burned surface is so smooth that it acts much like a mirror and reflects the image of objects easily. This is especially due to having a well-sanded surface and being gentle with the burner. If you press too hard, it can dent

the surface and destroy that glassy surface.

Don't Use the Tip

As mentioned above, the shading point is my favorite tip for creating a deep black value. However, don't apply downward pressure to the upper tip. There isn't much heat in that part, and it can easily be bent by excessive pressure. (Yep, that's the first thing I did when learning! My first shading point will forever resemble a banana.)

Use the "Heel"

Instead, focus slight downward pressure onto the "heel," or backside, of the shading point. This area holds more consistent heat and will transfer that heat to the wood much better. As mentioned above, use a "slight" downward pressure. Pushing too hard can cause denting of the wood, even with the heel, and result in a rough appearance. Overall, it's best to "float" the point across the wood and use heat instead of pressure to burn.

Tip Slow and steady is the best! Take your time and keep the point moving at all times. If you stop, the point can stick or grab the surface of the wood, peeling off the top layer or causing dents. Practice, practice, practice!

OPTIONS: There are other points that you can use instead of the shading point. These include spoon shaders, spear shaders, transfer points, and more. Experiment to see which one you like best.

Spoon shader   Spear shader   Transfer point

Practice: Other Options for Solid Blacks

There are many ways to burn a solid black value, and this section contains a couple more ideas to try. Oftentimes, I will use many of these options depending on the size and complexity of a subject, so it's helpful to learn them all.

Back and Forth
Use a larger tip, such as the flow point, and slowly burn a consistent back-and-forth motion.

Circles
Burn in a circular motion with a larger point and slowly fill in the area with a dark value.

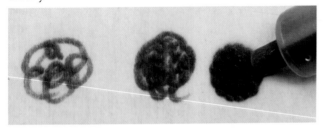

Stippling

Stippling is great for creating a dark value! Just slowly press the tip into the wood to create dark indentations.

Practice: Gradients

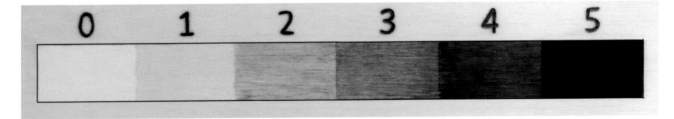

Gradients are a wonderful way to blend shaded areas for a seamless appearance. However, sometimes gradients can be a little daunting because there are so many different values that can be difficult to pinpoint. Therefore, one of the easiest ways to learn gradients is to create a value chart similar to the one pictured above. Our eyes may have trouble separating tiny fluctuations of value, but it's easier to break down the array of values into a few steps:

0. White pigment added after burning for extra depth.
1. Unburned wood
2. Light mid-tones
3. Mid-tones
4. Dark mid-tones
5. Darks

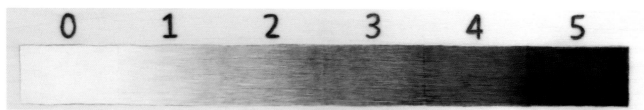

After creating a simple value chart, it's time to burn the gradient. Work off of the five values and slowly blend each zone together. As you blur the lines between values, you can see how each zone relates to one another. (For safety reasons, do not use your burner near any white pigment.)

When working on larger projects with multiple values, try to break down each area into the different values before blending them together to create seamless gradients.

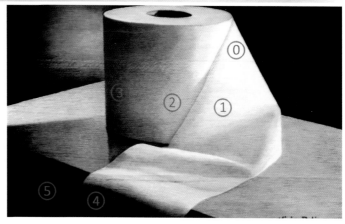

Removing Carbon Build-Up

Carbon is a by-product of burning any combustible material, and it can easily build up on your woodburning point. This can happen quickly when burning with a higher temperature. When carbon builds up on the point, you'll notice smudgy strokes and a definite loss of temperature. It's critical to remove this carbon while you work to ensure a more consistent burn.

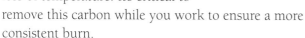

Removing Carbon

A quick and easy way to remove carbon from a point is to turn the temperature dial to max for about 30 seconds to burn it off. This works best with higher temperature burners like the Razertip and allows you to get back to work quickly. However, turning the temp up so high can possibly damage the point or the burner, so keep that in mind when burning off the carbon.

Another method is to rub the point on sandpaper to scrub off the carbon. If your sandpaper has a foam backing, turn the burner off and allow it to cool

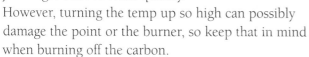

completely over several minutes. This will ensure that you don't burn into the foam and release potentially toxic fumes. Unfortunately, this can add significant time to your woodburning project.

One of the best ways to remove carbon from a point is to gently rub the point on a fine, wire mesh. In this example, I'm using a tea strainer. This method allows you to remove the carbon while you work without stressing the point with extreme temperatures or delaying progress by turning the burner off.

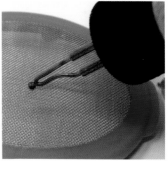

SAFETY

Tip This tea strainer has plastic edging. If you use one, it's imperative that you don't accidentally burn into the plastic.

Chapter 8
ADDING COLOR AND FINISHING

Adding color to a woodburning can be exciting! It's a great way to give pyrographic art a different dimension. The choice to add color is simply up to you and your preferences. Don't be afraid to try new combinations of colorful mediums to your woodburnings.

Please remember to wait until the burning is complete before adding color of any kind. Burning over any paints or pigments can produce potentially toxic fumes. Always protect your health first by adding color last.

When planning to use color, it's helpful to decide whether you want bold or more subtle coloring. I usually consider my subject when making this decision. If my woodburning includes a subject that is naturally very colorful, like a flower, then I'll add brighter and bolder colors. However, if my subject is naturally more neutral, such as animal fur, then I'll only add a touch of subtle coloring.

Bold color is achieved by using paints, including watercolors, acrylics, oils, inks, and markers.

Subtle color is created using colored pencils or very thin washes of paint.

Tip The heat from woodburning will burnish and seal off the wood fibers, which can make it difficult to add color. If you plan on adding color to a pyrography, try to avoid burning it too dark.

In the image to the right, I burned a test gradient on basswood, then applied different mediums over the top. As you can see, the darkest areas accept little to no pigment.

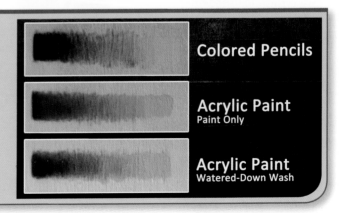

Colored Pencils

Acrylic Paint
Paint Only

Acrylic Paint
Watered-Down Wash

Acrylic Paint

Acrylic paint offers a great range of bold colors in an easy-to-use water-based medium. Acrylics tend to be quite opaque, but they can also be applied to a woodburning in thin, watered-down layers.

I don't pre-treat my woodburnings before adding acrylic paints. As long as you don't use too much water, there's very little risk of the wood swelling or cracking. Just paint directly onto the wood.

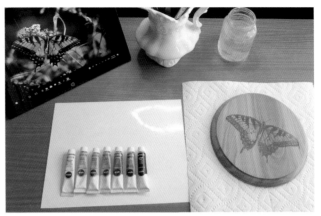

To paint on a woodburning, you would need acrylic paint, soft brushes, water, and a palette. For this example, I'm using a piece of glossy photo paper for an inexpensive palette.

Woodburning before paint

A little paint goes a long way, especially when thinning it with water. It's a good idea to experiment with acrylic paint on a scrap piece of wood before applying it to a woodburning. This helps to learn how to use the paint in watered-down layers.

Woodburning after paint

Acrylic paint dries very quickly, which allows for easy application of multiple layers.

Colored Pencils

Colored pencils are an easy way to add color without the setup and possible mess of using paints. They work best on mostly unburned wood, which allows the pigment from the pencils to adhere to the wood. There are many colored pencils on the market and most work fine on wood, although higher-quality pencils will definitely produce better results.

Before adding colored pencils, analyze the photo and select the colors you think you'll need. I'll often make a test scribble on a blank piece of paper first to be sure of the color.

To maintain the purity of the color, I often apply white first to the highlights and whitest areas.

Next, just color directly onto the wood. You can apply different layers of colors and blend them together quite easily. Remember that colored pencils can be quite subtle, so you may need to build up several layers. But overall, just experiment and have fun!

Watercolors

Watercolors are a great medium for free-flowing expression. The paint can be transparent or opaque and offers an interesting twist to a woodburning.

Using watercolors directly on untreated wood can be quite frustrating because the water and pigments immediately soak into the surface of the wood. This prevents the artist from being able to manipulate the watercolors, and worse yet, the water-soaked wood can swell and crack. But, with a few simple steps to prepare the wood, you can enjoy watercolors with woodburning.

For this example, I chose a simple subject that would work well with a visually interesting background. I wanted the viewer to recognize the watercolor medium, so I combined soft washes with hard-edged water lines.

The wood surface must be primed and sealed before using watercolors. I use Liquitex® Professional Clear Gesso because it dries translucent and offers a great "tooth" for holding the paint.

I applied a liquid masking fluid to protect the hummingbird woodburning before adding watercolors. This paints on in a liquid form and dries into a flexible sheet of latex.

Protect your workspace with paper towels or newspaper and elevate your project. I used paper cups as props under my woodburning. This keeps the project from sticking to the paper towels.

Pour a small amount of clear gesso onto the wood.

Spread the gesso out across the wood with a fine-bristle paintbrush. To maintain transparency, don't apply too much gesso. A thin, even layer works best.

Smooth out the random brush lines with even strokes.
Gesso must dry for at least 24 hours before painting.

After the wood surface has been primed and the gesso has dried for at least 24 hours, apply the liquid masking fluid to the hummingbird. All you need is your woodburning, liquid masking fluid, and a small paintbrush. (Keep in mind that the masking fluid will most likely adhere to the paintbrush bristles and ruin the brush.)

Dip the paintbrush into the masking fluid and apply it to the subject. Be very careful to follow the edges with precision and cover the subject with a thin layer.

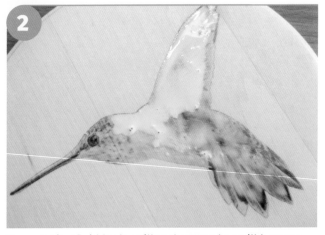

The masking fluid looks milky when wet but will become semi-transparent as it dries.

Once the masking fluid is completely dry, you can start painting.

Since this is a book about woodburning, I won't delve into the details of watercolor art. There are many wonderful books dedicated to watercolors, so I'll be showing a simple wash in this example. These are my supplies for the project; at the minimum you'll need watercolor paints, brushes, a palette, and water.

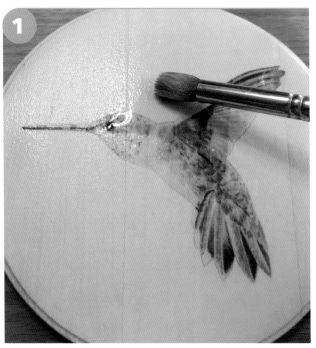

I planned on adding a wash behind the hummingbird, so I prepped the surface with a layer of water.

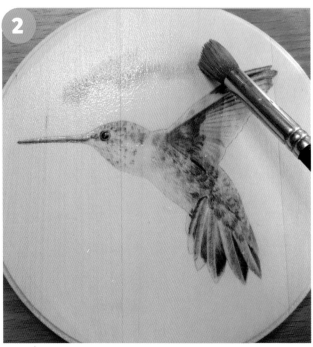

Apply your chosen colors for the wash. Control the transparency of the paints by adding more or less water.

Allow the watercolor wash to dry completely.

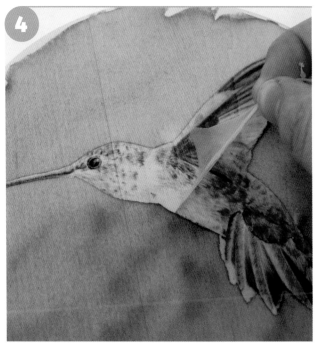

Using your finger, begin at the edge of the masking fluid and gently start pulling toward yourself until the masking fluid begins to roll up. Then you can carefully start peeling off the masking.

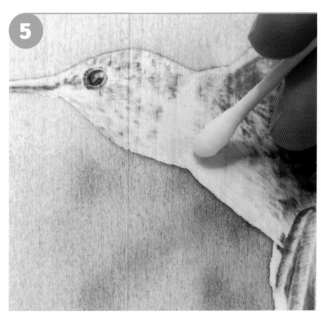

5

Use a wet cotton swab to clean up any paint that may have escaped onto the burning.

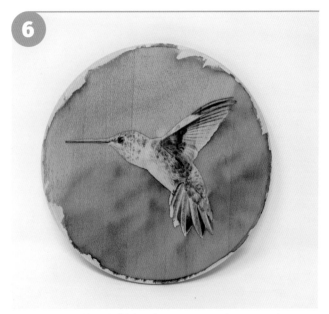

6

After the masking fluid has been removed, you can leave the woodburning as is.

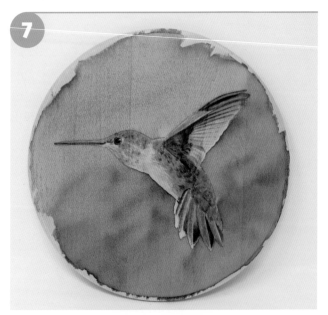

7

You can also apply watercolors to the hummingbird.

8

I wasn't quite happy with the light green background; I felt that the bird blended in too well. So, I re-masked the hummingbird and added a wash of purple to increase the contrast between the background and the bird.

9 Add a clear coat to protect the woodburning. I applied three coats of Polycrylic™ once the burning and painting is finished. I haven't had any problems with the paint running or bleeding when using this method; even so, I would recommend that you don't overbrush the first coat or use a spray-on finish. Feel free to substitute the clear coat of your choice.

It's important to protect and seal your finished woodburning. There are many great products on the market with multiple finishes, such as matte, semi-gloss, and glossy.

I used three coats of water-based Minwax® Polycrylic, then added one coat of Permalac® for UV protection. I encourage you to experiment with several options to see what works best for you.

Brush-On

Acrylic Paint

Colored Pencils

For most woodburnings I brush on three coats of Minwax Polycrylic, including the front, back, and sides. This works well for me on pyrographies without color and also when using acrylic paint or colored pencils.

Tip When applying the first coat over colored pencils, be careful not to overbrush or the colors might run and bleed.

SAFETY

Tip Always follow the product instructions carefully and wear appropriate safety equipment.

Spray-On

Water-based Markers

Watercolor Paint

If you have used strong colors on your woodburning, such as markers or water-based paints, it can be helpful to use a spray-on finish to avoid smearing the colors.

Tip Always experiment with new techniques and finishes on test pieces before using them on an important project.

UV Protection

Woodburning art can be quite sensitive to the harmful effects of the sun, so it's helpful to apply a UV protectant. Some finishes come complete with UV protection but can create a yellowing effect. Other products are non-yellowing but do not contain a UV protectant. Once again, feel free to experiment with different products.

Even with a UV protectant, I encourage artists and customers to hang their woodburning art away from direct sunlight. Some clear-coating products are advertised for "exterior" use and will help to protect the wood; however, most woodburnings can fade significantly if placed in direct sunlight.

Chapter 9

FIXING MISTAKES

"The easiest way to fix a mistake is by not making one in the first place." I often say this to myself when working because it reminds me to slow down, take my time, and plan my burning in a way that I don't create careless mistakes.

Tips for Preventing Mistakes
- **Physical factors:** Be mindful of how your body is feeling before and during woodburning. If you have a strong case of the caffeine jitters, it might be challenging to burn fine lines or intricate details. Weightlifting, sleepiness, exercising, drugs, or alcohol can cause similar problems. Try to burn when you are well rested and calm.
- **Emotional factors:** If you are angry, upset, or frustrated, it can be easy to press too hard and damage the surface of the wood or simply make an error. Do your best to woodburn when in a relaxed mental state so you can focus on your project.

Tip If you're unsure of a new point or technique, I strongly recommend keeping a scrap piece of wood nearby to test these practices before using them on your project. This also goes for large temperature adjustments.

Sandpaper

Even when being careful, mistakes happen sometimes. Sandpaper is a great way to "erase" mistakes or accidental burn marks. Try to use a fine-grit sandpaper if possible so you don't get large scratches on the wood surface. Remember that the lighter mistakes are easier to sand off, and you may need to do a lot of sanding to remove the darker burn marks.

Tip If you dig the burner down into the wood when burning, you may not be able to sand away mistakes.

Knife Blade

On occasions you can also scratch or scrape away mistakes with a knife blade or X-Acto® knife. This is helpful if you have a very small mistake to remove and you don't want to "erase" the surrounding areas.

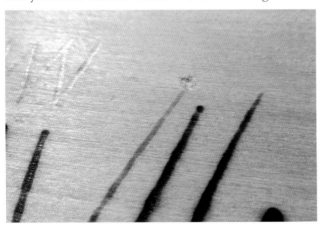

This method can easily create deep gouges and damage the wood surface, so exercise care and always be careful not to cut yourself.

Composition

Sometimes you can hide an error or mistake by changing the composition of your project. Try turning an accidental burn mark into a bird flying through the sky or burning dark grass over the top of a misshapen hoof. This can be tricky when trying to hide a really dark mistake but remember that this is an option.

Paint

Acrylic paint can be a fun way to cover over big mistakes since it can be quite opaque. In this example, I was unhappy with the rump of an elk I had burned, so I painted some foliage over the area. (Just be sure that you don't go back and burn over or near the paint; doing so could release potentially toxic fumes.)

Troubleshooting

Burner Does Not Make Marks

Make sure that your woodburning unit is plugged in and turned on. Remember that some units heat up very quickly, while others need about five minutes or so to reach optimal temperature. Make sure to double-check that your pen or point is fully inserted or tightened, and that the points are free of carbon. Occasionally, the mechanics within a woodburning unit can break or burn out, and you may need to have the unit professionally repaired or replaced, but this is quite rare.

Cannot Burn Darker Values

There are many things that can prevent a woodburning unit from burning the darker values, and here are a few to watch out for:

Temperature Dial

Sometimes it's easy to bump or dislodge the built-in temperature dial and accidentally reduce the heat. Double-check that the temperature dial is at the optimal setting. You can also tape or use rubber bands on the dial in place to prevent it from shifting by accident.

Carbon

Take a look at the point and see if there is a buildup of black carbon. Excessive carbon can prohibit the transfer of heat onto the wood, making it difficult to burn darker values. To remove the carbon, either turn up the burner and cook off the carbon or gently scrape/sand the carbon off the point. (For more information on cleaning points, please see page 43.)

Wind

The temperature of woodburning pens and units can fluctuate greatly in the wind. Try to work inside or seek shelter from the wind when burning outside. Electric fans, ceiling fans, swamp coolers, forced air vents, and open windows can all blow on the point and inadvertently pull heat from the woodburner.

Even something as simple as whistling while you woodburn can lower the temperature and make burning those darker values difficult.

Power

If your point is free of carbon, there's no wind blowing on the pen, and you're still having troubles burning darker values, you might check your power. Make sure that the woodburning unit is completely plugged in and that the cord isn't damaged. If you're using an extension cord or power strip, try to limit the number of other devices plugged into the same electrical outlet. For example, if an electric space heater is plugged in and running on the same outlet as your woodburning unit, then you'll notice a large drop in power and heat while burning.

Surface Material

Some materials for pyrography burn very easily at lower temperatures, while others don't. Surprisingly, watercolor paper can take a long time to burn to a dark value, and the same is true for burning on bone or skulls.

Mysterious Spots

Sometimes, when burning, you'll see a mysterious colored spot show up on the wood. This can be especially frustrating when burning lighter areas such as a face, etc. This can be due to tiny threads or bits of fabric that float through the air and land on your burning. Once the hot point goes across the threads, it burns out any pigment and adheres that to the wood surface. My mysterious spots are usually blue and come from the glove that I wear while working. Sometimes I can spot them sitting on the wood and brush them off, but other times I don't see them in time. To prevent this, be aware of your clothing and nearby fabrics that may be shedding on your work station. You can also occasionally wipe down your art while working with your hand. Keep in mind that unsanded wood tends to hold on to those pesky bits of threads and hair more, so always sand your wood before burning.

Chapter 10 PROJECTS

There are a wide variety of projects in this book, and they are organized into three different categories.

Level 1 Projects

These are great for the beginning artist with no experience with woodburning. They feature simple patterns that are burned with basic lines and minimal shading, as explained in the fundamentals section. Note that these easy projects can be embellished with colored pencils, paint, or even resin if you're feeling adventurous.

Level 2 Projects

These projects help the beginning artist to build off the fundamentals they have learned and incorporate elements of lines and shading, while exploring more complex designs. Some of these tutorials include extra options such as painting with watercolors or even creating jewelry.

Level 3 Projects

The projects in this level encourage the reader to move toward creating artwork with more shading and depth while relying less on basic lines. They also explore burning on different surfaces, such as boxes and frames, and incorporate options for adding color.

Suggested Points

Throughout the project sections I've included these suggested points. They are some of my favorite tips that I use on a regular basis. They work with either the Walnut Hollow Creative Versa-Tool or the Razertip burning units since those are the two systems that I use for my woodburning art. If you're not sure which point to use, then this can be a big help. Always remember that they are merely suggestions, and I encourage you to find the point that works best for you. If you don't have either of these burning systems, feel free to substitute the tip or nib of your choice.

Text and Outlines

1.5mm (1⁄16") Ball Stylus (Razertip)
Heat Level: 5–7

Mini Flow Point (Walnut Hollow Versa-Tool)
Heat Level: Max

Stippling

3mm (1⁄8") Ball Stylus (Razertip)
Heat Level: 5–7

Flow Point (Walnut Hollow Versa-Tool)
Heat Level: Max

Shading

Medium Spoon Shader (Razertip)
Heat Level: 5–10

Shading Point (Walnut Hollow Versa-Tool)
Heat Level: Orange–Max

Fine Lines

1.5mm (1⁄16") Ball Stylus (Razertip)
Heat Level: 5–7

Shading Point (Walnut Hollow Versa-Tool)
Heat Level: Orange–Max

Extra Fine Lines

Medium Knife (Razertip)
Heat Level: 4–7

Shading Point (Walnut Hollow Versa-Tool)
Heat Level: Orange–Max

Blocking In Areas

3mm (1⁄8") Ball Stylus (Razertip)
Heat Level: 5–7

Flow Point (Walnut Hollow Versa-Tool)
Heat Level: Max

Blocking In Small Areas

1.5mm (1⁄16") Ball Stylus (Razertip)
Heat Level: 5–7

Mini Flow Point (Walnut Hollow Versa-Tool)
Heat Level: Max

Level 1 Project:

BOOKMARK

Materials

- Unfinished wooden bookmark (approximately 1.25" x 4.75" [3 x 12cm])
- Pattern (see page 129)
- Graphite paper and red pen (To transfer the image)
- Fine-grit sandpaper (to sand graphite lines and fix errors)
- Woodburning unit
- Woodburning pens or points

Optional

- Colored pencils
- Bookmark tassel
- Clear coat sealant

Suggested Tips

Text and Outlines

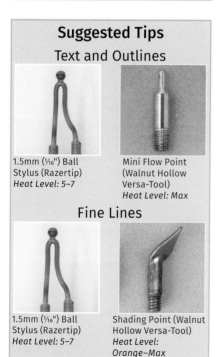

1.5mm (¹⁄₁₆") Ball Stylus (Razertip)
Heat Level: 5–7

Mini Flow Point (Walnut Hollow Versa-Tool)
Heat Level: Max

Fine Lines

1.5mm (¹⁄₁₆") Ball Stylus (Razertip)
Heat Level: 5–7

Shading Point (Walnut Hollow Versa-Tool)
Heat Level: Orange–Max

I found these cute little wooden bookmarks online. They were quite thin, so it was important not to burn too deeply. This is a simple design that features text, basic lines, and a little shading on the arrow.

Begin by using a small point to burn the text. (Remember, don't press too hard on this thin piece of wood.)

Next, use a fine point to burn a basic line over the guidelines for the arrow.

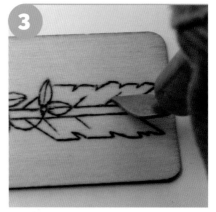

Continue burning over the graphite transfer lines and create an even line for the vine and leaves. Feel free to turn the wood to make burning straight lines easier.

Turn the shading point over and use the upper tip to burn fine lines as veins on the leaves. (You can also use an alternate small point.)

You can use a small point to add a little shading on one side of the arrow and the edges of the arrowhead. Burn fine lines on the feathers, with a little shading where the feathers are attached to the wooden shaft.

Color Option!

Attach a colored tassel through the pre-drilled hole and add some colored pencils.

Seal the wood with a clear coat of your choice.

Option: Add colored pencils.

Level 1 Project:

WELCOME SIGN

This is a great beginner project that features a simple design, plus a fun introduction to shading.

Materials
- Unfinished wooden plaque (approximately 13" x 5.25" [33 x 13cm])
- Pattern (see page 133)
- Graphite paper and red pen (to transfer the image)
- Fine-grit sandpaper (to sand graphite lines and fix errors)
- Woodburning unit
- Woodburning pens or points

Optional
- Colored pencils
- Spray or brush-on clear coat sealant

Suggested Tips

Text and Outlines

1.5mm (¹⁄₁₆") Ball Stylus (Razertip)
Heat Level: 5–7

Mini Flow Point (Walnut Hollow Versa-Tool)
Heat Level: Max

Shading

Medium Spoon Shader (Razertip)
Heat Level: 5–10

Shading Point (Walnut Hollow Versa-Tool)
Heat Level: Orange–Max

1 Begin by burning the "Welcome" text with a small or medium sized burning point. Then turn the burner to a medium or high heat (depending on your burner of choice) and gently burn the outlines of the design.

2 Next, continue burning simple lines for the rest of the design.

3 Use a shading point or smaller tip to add a little shading to the design. I like to add darker values where elements seem to overlap, as well as on lower edges such as the bottom of branches and flowers.

COLOR OPTION!

Use a shading point or flatter tip to burn a dark value around the beveled edge of the wood and add colored pencils to the design. (During this project, I changed my mind and added the woodburned border after applying the color. Normally, I strongly advice against adding color until the burn is complete due to the possibility of accidentally burning the pigments, which could release toxic fumes. But the color was quite far from the border, which made it safer to burn the edging. When recreating this project, I suggest burning the border before adding color.)

After the project is complete and dried (if painted), seal the wood with either a spray-on or brushed clear coat.

Level 1 Project:

MOUNTAIN BANGLE BRACELET

I usually burn on flat surfaces, but this 3D project was a blast! It features a very simple design with a mountain range and solid black values.

Materials

- Unfinished wooden bangle (approximately 10.75" x 1.5" [27 x 4cm])
- Pattern (see page 129)
- Graphite paper and red pen (to transfer the image)
- Fine-grit sandpaper (to sand graphite lines and fix errors)
- Woodburning unit
- Woodburning pens or points

Optional

- Paintbrushes
- Acrylic paint
- Spray finish

1.5mm (¹⁄₁₆") Ball Stylus (Razertip) *Heat Level: 5–7*

Mini Flow Point (Walnut Hollow Versa-Tool) *Heat Level: Max*

3mm (¹⁄₈") Ball Stylus (Razertip) *Heat Level: 5–7*

Flow Point (Walnut Hollow Versa-Tool) *Heat Level: Max*

1

It can be a little tricky to work on a rounded surface, but it helps to trim away any excess paper above the mountains. Wrap the reference photo around the bangle and secure it with tape. Slip the corner of the graphite paper underneath and transfer the pattern a little bit at a time.

2

After transferring the pattern onto the wood, use a small point on a medium to high temperature and burn a solid black line over the graphite marks. Remember to burn slowly and steadily, with a light pressure.

3

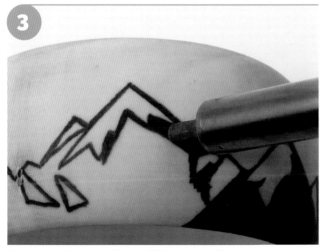

Next, use a larger point to fill in the outlined areas.

4

Continue burning until all of the mountains are blocked in with a dark, black value.

Color Option!

If you'd like to color to your bangle bracelet, you might have fun with this starry gradient. I used acrylic paint straight from the tube. Since we don't add extra water, it's not critical to gesso the wood before applying paint. Just paint directly onto the wood, but be aware that acrylic paint dries within a few minutes, so continue to work steadily.

Use a small paintbrush to apply a layer of purple at the top of the bracelet. It's helpful to keep the bottom edge of purple lighter and irregular.

Apply an orange color to the lower part of the sky with a small paintbrush. Be careful to keep the acrylic paint off the burned mountains.

Paint the middle of the sky with a magenta and blend it into the orange at the bottom and the purple above.

4

You can add more of the three colors if needed to blend them into a gradient.

5

Add stars to the bangle by carefully applying white paint with a fine paintbrush. To create brighter stars, use more paint, and then use less paint to create the dimmer stars. Usually the stars will appear lighter toward the mountains.

6

Once the painting is complete and thoroughly dried, you can seal it with a spray finish.

Acrylic paint: I used Liquitex BASICS® brand paint, but any acrylic paint can be substituted. Keep in mind that cheaper paints tend to be watered down and may appear more transparent.

Level 1 Project:

SNOWFLAKE COASTERS

These simple snowflake coasters are a great beginner project and will teach you how to burn on an end-grain piece of wood. Birch rounds may be harder than basswood, but they don't contain sap like pine, so they are a great middle-road wood to try.

Materials
- Unfinished wooden birch rounds (approximately 3.5" x 3.5" [9 x 9cm])
- Pattern (see page 130)
- Graphite paper and red pen (to transfer the image)
- Fine-grit sandpaper (to sand graphite lines and fix errors)
- Woodburning unit
- Woodburning pens or points

Optional
- Clear gesso
- Paintbrushes
- Watercolor paint
- Resin
- Paper cup
- Wooden stick or gloves
- Glue-on felt pads
- Screw-eye
- Ribbon

1

Using a small woodburning point on a medium temperature, focus on the basic structure of each snowflake and burn the simple lines. Be sure to use a light and even pressure while "floating" the point across the surface of the wood.

2

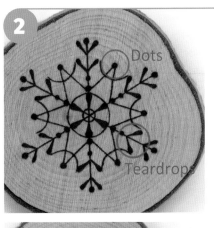
Dots
Teardrops

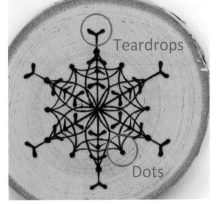
Teardrops
Dots

Teardrops
Dots

Dots
Teardrops

Suggested Tips
Text and Outlines

1.5mm (¹⁄₁₆") Ball Stylus (Razertip)
Heat Level: 5–7

Mini Flow Point (Walnut Hollow Versa-Tool)
Heat Level: Max

Tip If you press too hard when burning lines, the point can dig into the wood, causing uneven lines or overburn.

The burner can sink down in between the grain, then raise back up again. This makes lines look narrow in one area but wider in another.

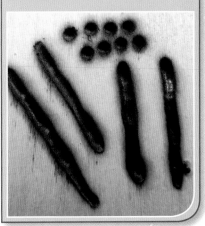

Add embellishments to each simple design, such as teardrop shapes on the outer edges and dots where points come together. Feel free to be creative with this step!

Color Option!

If you'd like to add watercolor paint to the coasters, it's important to pre-treat them with clear gesso first.

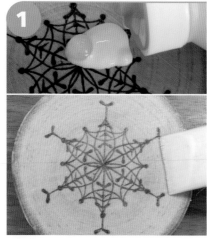

Apply a small amount of clear gesso on each coaster and spread it around with a smooth paintbrush. **Allow the gesso to dry for at least 24 hours.**

After the gesso has dried, you can begin painting. For this project, I wanted the woodburning to stand out, so I kept the paint on the outer edges. Pre-wet the wood and apply water all across the surface of each coaster.

While the coaster is still wet, use a small brush to "drop" blue paint along the outer edge and allow the paint to bleed toward the center. Feel free to pick up the coaster and tip it from side to side to help the paint to flow. Keep in mind that the paint will dry lighter than it appears.

Resin Option

Option: Give your coasters a polished, wintery feeling by adding watercolor paint and sealing with resin.

Allow the painted coasters to dry for a few days. Then prop each coaster up on a paper cup and pour resin over the top to protect the coasters. Use a wooden stick or gloved fingers to spread the resin on the outer edges for a smooth finish. (Note: Always follow the directions and precautions that come with your choice of resin.)

After the resin has cured, sand any drips from the bottom and apply glue-on felt pads.

Creative Option

Instead of coasters, attach a metal screw-eye into the top of each piece and tie on a ribbon to create festive ornaments.

FUN AND FOXY KEYCHAIN

This keychain is a very simple design with the added twist of a functional project. If you are just beginning, use the pattern to create a cute piece of art that stands alone. But if you're feeling adventuresome, try attaching this pretty fox to a key ring for fun on the go.

Materials

- Unfinished wooden teardrop tags (approximately 1.5" x 2.25" [4 x 6cm])
- Pattern (see page 129)
- Graphite paper and red pen (to transfer the image)
- Fine-grit sandpaper (to sand graphite lines and fix errors)
- Woodburning unit
- Woodburning pens or points
- Two sets of pliers
- Key ring
- Jump ring (approximately 10 mm)

Optional

- Colored pencils
- Spray or brush-on finish

Suggested Tips

Text and Outlines

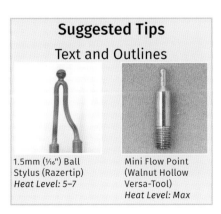

1.5mm (¹⁄₁₆") Ball Stylus (Razertip) *Heat Level: 5–7*

Mini Flow Point (Walnut Hollow Versa-Tool) *Heat Level: Max*

1

Since the keychain is so small, it helps to use a fine-sized pen or point to burn the text. Keep your heat on the medium side to prevent accidental overburn.

2

Use a small point and a medium temperature to burn the outlines of the fox design. Remember to maintain a light pressure and use gentle transitions on and off the wood to avoid stop spots.

3

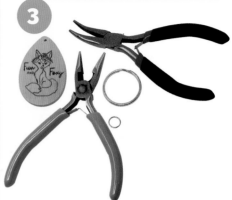

To assemble your keychain, you'll need two sets of needle-nosed pliers, a 10mm jump ring, a key ring, and your custom wooden fob. (It's okay if your tools don't look the same as pictured.)

4

When using a jump ring, never pull each side open horizontally, like opening a bag of chips. This will distort and damage the metal. Instead, use two pliers and twist the left side forward and the right side backward. This creates an "S" shape that allows the jump ring to open safely.

5

Once the jump ring is open, place the wooden fob and the key ring inside the opened jump ring.

6

Reverse the process and close the jump ring by twisting the left side backward and the right side forward.

Color Option!

If you want to add a little color to your keychain woodburning, apply white colored pencils to the face, ears, chest, and tail of the fox. Use sienna brown for the fur and add some pinks and reds to the floral crown.

Seal the wood with a spray or gentle brush-on finish.

COFFEE TIME

This project features a simple design with the fun twist of working with negative space. It's also a great opportunity to practice burning black backgrounds. (You can choose to substitute a simpler option by burning the coffee cup and text instead, and leave the background unburned.)

Materials
- Unfinished wooden plaque (approximately 5" x 7" [13 x 18cm])
- Pattern (see page 132)
- Graphite paper and red pen (to transfer the image)
- Fine-grit sandpaper (to sand graphite lines and fix errors)
- Woodburning unit
- Woodburning pens or points

Optional
- Colored pencils or acrylic paint
- Spray or brush-on finish

Use a medium point on a higher heat to burn a dark outline around the design. (If you don't want to burn the background, just fill in the design with a dark black and you're finished. But if you want a black background, then proceed with the next step.)

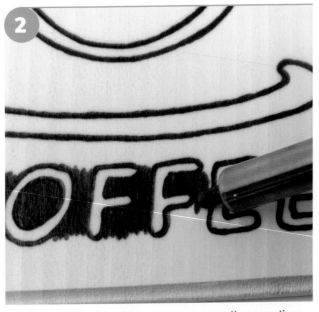

To burn dark black in tight areas, use a small- or medium-sized tip, such as the flow point, and slowly burn back and forth. (You can also use a circular method or even burn with stippling.)

For this example, I wanted a smooth surface, so I used the shading point for most of background. However, it can be tricky to fit in tight areas, so use the flow point to block in the smaller areas of the design.

After the tight areas are blocked in, switch to the shading point and use the upper tip to burn an outline around the initial design. (This creates a heat buffer to prevent accidental overburn and ghosting later.)

5

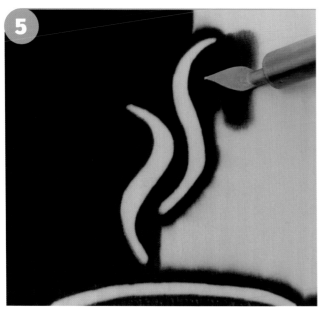

Next, use the shading point flat on the wood and slowly burn back and forth to create a deep black value. Burn with the grain if possible, and work in small sections.

6

After the background is filled in, you can either add color or seal the wood.

Color Option!

Apply colored pencils or acrylic paint if you want to add color to your coffee woodburning.

Seal the wood with a spray or gentle brush-on finish.

Level 1 Project:
WOLF GRADIENT

This wolf woodburning is a great project to practice the 5-Step Shading Scale and to see it in use. There are five distinct values in this piece: the unburned wood, light midtones, midtones, dark midtones, and darks. With these five shades, you can create a sense of distance and atmosphere within the piece. I made this woodburning on cherry wood, so the lighter values have a natural reddish hue. Feel free to substitute the wood of your choice or use this pattern to learn about different types of wood.

Materials
- Unfinished wooden cherry round (approximately 8" x 8" [20 x 20cm])
- Pattern (see page 133)
- Graphite paper and red pen (to transfer the image)
- Fine-grit sandpaper (to sand graphite lines and fix errors)
- Woodburning unit
- Woodburning pens or points

Text and Outlines		Blocking In Areas		Shading	
1.5mm (¹⁄₁₆") Ball Stylus (Razertip) *Heat Level: 5–7*	Mini Flow Point (Walnut Hollow Versa-Tool) *Heat Level: Max*	3mm (¹⁄₈") Ball Stylus (Razertip) *Heat Level: 5–7*	Flow Point (Walnut Hollow Versa-Tool) *Heat Level: Max*	Medium Spoon Shader (Razertip) *Heat Level: 5–10*	Shading Point (Walnut Hollow Versa-Tool) *Heat Level: Orange–Max*

- Unburned Wood (Level 1)
- Light Midtones (Level 2)
- Midtones (Level 3)
- Dark Midtones (Level 4)
- Darks (Level 5)

Example of 5-Step Shading

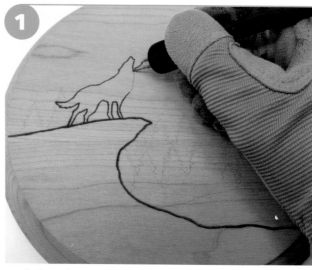

Begin by using a smaller sized pen or point to burn a dark outline around the silhouette of the wolf and hillside.

Next, fill in the wolf with a solid black. Since the wolf has narrow areas, such as the legs and tail, use a smaller point (flow point) to maintain better control.

For the larger area of hillside, use the shading point flat on the wood to create a dark black burn.

Next, begin burning the darker midtones on the small hill in the middle area. It's okay to start out light and build your shading in layers. This is a great way to ensure that you don't get an area too dark.

Tip When burning the trees, I find it helpful to turn the wood sideways and use a back-and-forth or up-and-down type of motion. I wanted to create shading only, with no texture to the trees. You might try burning both ways and see what works best for you.

Finish shading the darker mid-tones. Make the area as smooth and even as possible by burning multiple layers and blending them together.

Burn the first row of trees with a mid-tone value. It's okay to turn down the temperature of the burner at this point to give you more control.

Finish by burning the second row of trees with a light mid-tone value. I would strongly recommend turning the burner down for this step.

Level 2 Project:
MANDALA

Mandalas are beautifully symmetrical and embody a sense of peace. This project incorporates a variety of textures and is a great exercise in basic lines and gradients using stippling.

Materials

- Unfinished wooden plaque (approximately 11" x 11" [28 x 28cm])
- Pattern (see page 134)
- Graphite paper and red pen (to transfer the image)
- Fine-grit sandpaper (to sand graphite lines and fix errors)
- Woodburning unit
- Woodburning pens or points

Optional

- Colored pencils

Suggested Tips

Text and Outlines

1.5mm (1/16") Ball Stylus (Razertip)
Heat Level: 5–7

Mini Flow Point (Walnut Hollow Versa-Tool)
Heat Level: Max

Blocking In Areas

3mm (1/8") Ball Stylus (Razertip)
Heat Level: 5–7

Flow Point (Walnut Hollow Versa-Tool)
Heat Level: Max

1

Start in the center with a small point and carefully burn the flower and center pattern, including the lines and dots in the inner circle. Turn the wood as needed to better suit your hand position while burning. Use a light and even pressure during burning to create the finer lines. Pressing too hard or using too much heat can cause uneven lines and a ghosting overburn.

2

Burn the outline of the middle circle using a small point with medium to high heat, depending on your woodburning tool. Sometimes it can help to burn curves in shorter strokes.

3

Fill in the inner petals with a solid black burn. You can continue to use a small point, or switch to a medium-sized one to cover more ground.

4

Use a small point to add a stippling gradient to the middle petals and a solid black on the outer petals.

5 Burn an outline around the middle section of the design. Take your time to keep the lines as smooth as possible.

6 Fill in the middle areas with a solid, deep black. Feel free to switch to a larger point during this step. Keep in mind that carbon will build up on the point, so allow it to burn off or scrape it on a metal mesh to maintain a consistent temperature.

7 Switch back to a smaller point and outline the outer edges of the design.

8 Add a stippling gradient to the outer flowers and the flower buds.

COLOR OPTION!

The idea of a mandala offers a sense of peace and balance, so I chose to use the full spectrum of the rainbow to add color to this woodburning. Over the years, I have developed a love of creating unique images based on the rules of the rainbow. To this day, I love seeing the full spectrum of colors on a piece of art.

Level 2 Project:

ADVENTURE KEY HOLDER

I love this project because it can be so versatile. The design works great as a simple woodburned plaque, or even as a colorful inspirational piece. You can also install some cup hooks and create a functional key holder to encourage your daily adventures.

Materials
- Unfinished wood (approximately 10" x 8" [25 x 20cm])
- Pattern (see page 135)
- Graphite paper and red pen (to transfer the image)
- Fine-grit sandpaper (to sand graphite lines and fix errors)
- Woodburning unit
- Woodburning pens or points
- Sharp awl
- Hammer
- Screw-in cup hooks

Optional
- Watercolor paints
- Paintbrushes
- Clear gesso
- Spray finish

Suggested Tips

Text and Outlines

1.5mm (¹⁄₁₆") Ball Stylus (Razertip)
Heat Level: 5–7

Mini Flow Point (Walnut Hollow Versa-Tool)
Heat Level: Max

Blocking In Areas

3mm (¹⁄₈") Ball Stylus (Razertip)
Heat Level: 5–7

Flow Point (Walnut Hollow Versa-Tool)
Heat Level: Max

1 Use a small woodburning point on a medium/high heat to outline all the key elements of the design.

2 Burn a solid black within the border and mountains with a medium-sized point on a higher heat.

COLOR OPTION!

If you'd like to add watercolor paint to the plaque, it's important to pre-treat it with clear gesso first.

Tip Acrylic paint can be substituted for the watercolors. In this case, no gesso is needed.

1 Apply a small amount of clear gesso on the surface of the wood and spread it around with a smooth paintbrush. **Allow the gesso to dry for at least 24 hours.**

2 After the gesso has dried, have fun applying watercolor paints to the design. I added a gradient wash of reds and yellows to the background, a hint of steel blue to the mountains, and an exciting, vibrant blue banner.

3 Once the watercolors have dried, gently tap a sharp awl into each hook location with a small hammer. This helps the cup-hooks to start more easily.

4 Carefully screw in each cup-hook into the pre-awled holes.

Level 2 Project:

ALWAYS BEE KIND

Cherry is a blast to burn on and smells very nice. This wood burns the darker values quite easily, so if you plan on adding color later, avoid burning the lighter mid-tones. I love applying color to cherry because of the vivid contrast.

Suggested Tips

Text and Outlines

1.5mm (1⁄16") Ball Stylus (Razertip)
Heat Level: 5–7

Mini Flow Point (Walnut Hollow Versa-Tool)
Heat Level: Max

Shading

Medium Spoon Shader (Razertip)
Heat Level: 5–10

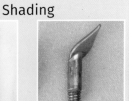

Shading Point (Walnut Hollow Versa-Tool)
Heat Level: Orange–Max

1

Use a small point on a medium/high heat to burn the word "Always."

2

If you want crisper edges on small text, try using the Walnut Hollow Creative Versa-Tool and shading point. Rock the woodburning tool upward and use the leading edge of the shading point to burn the intricate lettering.

3

Burn a simple outline around the flowers using a small point and a medium/high heat.

4

Use a shading point on medium/high heat to burn the darkest areas of the flowers. Work slowly to avoid overburn.

5

Continue using a shading point to burn the middle values of the flowers. Turn your burner down a little for the lighter values. If you plan on adding color, then leave the lightest areas unburned. This helps the paint or colored pencils adhere to the wood better.

6

Start working on the bees by burning the darkest values first with a small point.

7

Continue burning the bees by shading the mid-tones and adding fur strokes to create the fuzzy areas.

8

Complete the woodburning by adding the lighter mid-tones to the bees.

Always Bee Kind 83

Color Option!

1 Apply white colored pencil to the wings, eye, and highlights of each bee.

2 Continue by coloring the flowers and bees with a pale yellow.

3 Use an orange-colored pencil on the flowers and bees to build depth.

Complete the project by adding green to the leaves and buds. Seal your woodburning with a spray-on finish and UV protectant.

Level 2 Project:

FEATHER PENDANTS

The art of woodburning isn't limited to burning on wood. Watercolor paper can be a wonderful and versatile replacement for solid wood, and these cute pendants show that art can be fashionable as well. While the woodburning part of this project is quite simple, it helps you to learn how watercolor paper responds to a woodburning tool.

Materials
- Watercolor paper (hot pressed, 140 pound [63.5kg])
- Pattern (see page 129)
- Graphite paper and red pen (to transfer the image)
- Fine-grit sandpaper (to sand graphite lines and fix errors)
- Woodburning unit
- Woodburning pens or points
- Scissors
- Tape
- Glass cabochon (approximately 1.5" x 0.75" [4 x 2cm])
- Double-sided tape
- Craft glue
- Metal bezel (to fit the rectangular cabochon listed above)
- Jump ring (8mm)
- Necklace cord

Optional
- Watercolor paints
- Paintbrushes

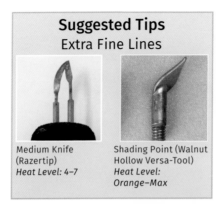

1

I find that it's easier to work on all four feather pendants together on a single piece of large paper. This makes it easier to handle instead of working on four tiny pieces of paper.

Since watercolor paper is quite thin, you can accidentally burn your table, so tape the watercolor paper onto a piece of unfinished wood before burning. If you've never burned on paper before, try experimenting with different woodburning points first on a scrap piece of paper.

2

Use a small and fine point on medium/high heat to burn the outlines of each feather. Be careful not to press too hard or burn through the paper.

Color Option!

Feel free to add watercolor paint or colored pencils to the feathers, or skip this step and continue on. Allow the watercolors to dry completely.

3

Create extra depth on the feathers by burning more lines inside of the outlines.

4

Use the four dots in each corner as a guide to carefully cut out each feather artwork.

5

Cut a piece of double-sided tape slightly larger than each pendant. Carefully peel off one side of the tape and press it firmly onto each paper. Turn it over and rub the backside of the paper with a fingernail or spoon to help the tape adhere to the paper and remove air bubbles. (I used heavy-duty double-sided tape from Gorilla®. The tape was quite thick and more than I needed for this project. Feel free to use normal double-sided tape instead.)

6

With a sharp pair of scissors, carefully trim the excess tape around the edges of each watercolor paper.

7

Remove the backing from the tape and carefully press the feather project onto the backside of a clear, rectangular cabochon. Rub the backside again with your fingernail or a spoon to press out any trapped air.

8

Trim any edges again with scissors if needed.

9

Apply a moderate amount of craft glue on the bezel (I used Aleene's® All Purpose Tacky Glue).

Set the pendant on a level surface to dry, then use a jump ring to attach the artwork to a necklace cord of your choice.

Pick up the pendant from the ends and gently press the flat side of the cabochon into the bezel tray.

10

Feather Pendants   **87**

Level 2 Project:
SERVING TRAY

Wooden serving trays come in a variety of sizes and offer a unique surface for woodburning. This project uses simple design lines but also allows you to practice shading too.

Materials
- Unfinished wooden serving tray (inside dimensions 13" x 9.5" [33 x 24cm])
- Pattern (see page 137)
- Graphite paper and red pen (to transfer the image)
- Fine-grit sandpaper (to sand graphite lines and fix errors)
- Woodburning unit
- Woodburning pens or points

Optional
- Colored pencils

Suggested Tips

Text and Outlines		Shading	
1.5mm (1/16") Ball Stylus (Razertip) *Heat Level: 5–7*	Mini Flow Point (Walnut Hollow Versa-Tool) *Heat Level: Max*	Medium Spoon Shader (Razertip) *Heat Level: 5–10*	Shading Point (Walnut Hollow Versa-Tool) *Heat Level: Orange–Max*

1

Start by outlining the text on the serving tray with a small point and moderate heat. Outlining text can help to create a cleaner edge before filling it in.

2

Use a small- or medium-sized point to fill in the text. Remember to regulate the temperature of your burner so you don't burn too hot and leave overburn or ghosting around the text.

3

Use a small, fine point and medium heat to burn a light outline around the main elements. For this example, I used the upper tip of the shading point that comes with the Walnut Hollow Creative Versa-Tool, and the heat was set at mid-orange.

Burn the darkest areas of the design with a small or medium point on a medium/high heat. It's okay to build up the darkest values by burning multiple layers to help avoid any overburn.

Next, burn the mid-tones of the design. Continue using your small/medium point to burn the middle values. Blend these areas into the darkest values as needed.

Finish the birdhouse by adding shading to the roof and sides. Burn streaks on the front of the birdhouse to mimic wood grain.

Tip Adding a darker edge on one side of each twig can give them a more rounded appearance.

7

Create the plaid heart by lightly burning every other row and column. Then burn every other square a bit more to create the plaid.

8

Burn the leaves of the design using darker mid-tones with more black at the tips of each leaf. Complete the design by burning the remaining flowers.

9

Complete the design by burning the remaining flowers.

Color Option!

Give this serving tray a springtime feel by adding colored pencils to the woodburning.

Level 3 Project:

FAMILY FRAME

This family frame is a wonderful opportunity to combine a flourished design with simple shading to create an elegant result.

Materials
- Unfinished wooden frame (approximately 9.5" x 7.5" [24 x 19cm])
- Pattern (see page 140)
- Graphite paper and red pen (to transfer the image)
- Fine-grit sandpaper (to sand graphite lines and fix errors)
- Woodburning unit
- Woodburning pens or points

Suggested Tips

Text and Outlines		Blocking In Areas		Shading	

1.5mm (¹⁄₁₆") Ball Stylus (Razertip) *Heat Level: 5–7*

Mini Flow Point (Walnut Hollow Versa-Tool) *Heat Level: Max*

3mm (⅛") Ball Stylus (Razertip) *Heat Level: 5–7*

Flow Point (Walnut Hollow Versa-Tool) *Heat Level: Max*

Medium Spoon Shader (Razertip) *Heat Level: 5–10*

Shading Point (Walnut Hollow Versa-Tool) *Heat Level: Orange–Max*

Tip Frames can be a bit challenging to burn on because of the hollow center. So, if you turn the frame over and insert a piece of wood on the backside, then you can fill the empty void and have a better surface for wrist support while working.

1

Use a small point on a medium temperature to burn an even line over the basic design

2

Continue using that small or medium point to burn the straight lines of the inner border. Remember to take your time and burn the lines as evenly as possibly.

3

Burn the word "Family" with a small or fine point.

4

Burn the inside of each flower and add a little shading or fine lines to the petals.

5

Use a shading point or fine tip to add a bit of shading to each leaf. You can even burn more tiny lines to create veins on the leaves.

6

Burn to a dark black with a small point on the corner designs, including the shadows under each flourish.

7

Also burn around the leaves and add shadows to the upper flourish.

8

Use a small or fine point to burn within the straight lines of the inner border.

9

Next use a shading point to add a little depth to the scroll and flourish border. For this project, I tried to imagine a light source shining down from the upper edge of the frame, and this image helped me to burn mid-tones on the lower edges of the design. I also added more darker mid-tones where scrolls might join together to give the image more depth.

10

Burn a slight gradient on the family plaque. Use a shading point and burn a dark mid-tone on the inner edge of the plaque, then slowly burn lighter toward the center.

11

Create a beveled appearance on the inner frame by burning a mid-tone on each size of the center void.

12

Remove the center wood support, seal the frame, and insert a family photo of your choice. (You can also add color if desired.)

Level 3 Project:

COUNTRY JAR

I found these cute wooden cutouts online and thought they would make a unique woodburning. The wood is quite thin, so be sure that you don't burn too deeply.

Materials
- Unfinished wooden jar cutout (approximately 7.5" x 12" [19 x 30cm])
- Pattern (see page 131)
- Graphite paper and red pen (to transfer the image)
- Fine-grit sandpaper (to sand graphite lines and fix errors)
- Woodburning unit
- Woodburning pens or points

Optional
- Colored pencils

Suggested Tips

Text and Outlines		Shading	
1.5mm (¹⁄₁₆") Ball Stylus (Razertip) *Heat Level: 5–7*	Mini Flow Point (Walnut Hollow Versa-Tool) *Heat Level: Max*	Medium Spoon Shader (Razertip) *Heat Level: 5–10*	Shading Point (Walnut Hollow Versa-Tool) *Heat Level: Orange–Max*

1

Outline the text and heart with a small, fine point. This can help your text to have crisper edges and look cleaner.

2

Fill in the outlined text with a small- or medium-sized point. (Remember, don't press too hard or you could damage the wood and/or point.)

3

Continue using a small point and burn an even outline around all of the design elements (except for the shading on the jar).

4

Begin adding embellishments to the design by burning fine lines on the flower petals.

5

Add shading to the flower with a shading point. Each petal is a little darker on the edges, and you can make shadows between the petals for more depth.

6

Next, burn the shading on the heart. The edges are a bit darker and the heart is lighter in the middle.

7

Burn the butterfly with a small point. The body and the outer edges of the wings are a dark value and create dark outlines for the veins of the wings. Add some lighter mid-tones to the closest wing and mid-tones to the other wings. Don't forget to add a little shadow underneath the closest wing for more depth.

8

Using the tip of your choice, burn the darkest areas of the ribbon around the neck of the jar.

9 Burn a dark value on the stems and bottom edges of the berries.

10 Fill in the berries with a circular gradient and blend it into the lower edge to create a rounded appearance.

11 Add some lighter shading to the tiny leaves, with a few shadows on the lower edges.

12 Use a shading point to burn the mid-tones of the ribbon.

13

14

15

These next few steps can be fun and abstract in nature. We'll be adding shading to the jar itself in the attempt to make it look like glass. Don't get too caught up with the exact shapes, just do your best and have fun! Start by burning the darkest values of the jar with the point of your choice.

Next, burn the mid-tones and blend them into the darker values.

Lastly, blend everything together by adding lighter mid-tones and creating smooth gradients and transitions throughout the jar.

Color Option!

If you'd like to add a little color, try using colored pencils to give your woodburning a little pop.

Level 3 Project:

MEMORY BOX

I loved the idea of creating an old-fashioned memory box with a woodburned lock and key, and the corner brackets add a touch of realism. Burning on boxes is a lot of fun, and sometimes includes a little more pre-planning to ensure that everything lines up properly, especially on the corners.

Materials
- Unfinished wooden box (approximately 10⅝" W x 7⅛" D x 2⁵⁄₁₆" H [27 x 18 x 6cm])
- Pattern (see page 138–139)
- Graphite paper and red pen (to transfer the image)
- Fine-grit sandpaper (to sand graphite lines and fix errors)
- Woodburning unit
- Woodburning pens or points

Optional
- Colored pencils

Suggested Tips

Text and Outlines

1.5mm (¹⁄₁₆") Ball Stylus (Razertip) *Heat Level: 5–7*	Mini Flow Point (Walnut Hollow Versa-Tool) *Heat Level: Max*

Shading

Medium Spoon Shader (Razertip) *Heat Level: 5–10*	Shading Point (Walnut Hollow Versa-Tool) *Heat Level: Orange–Max*

1 Begin by using a small point on medium to high heat and burn the basic lines of the corner brackets and screwheads.

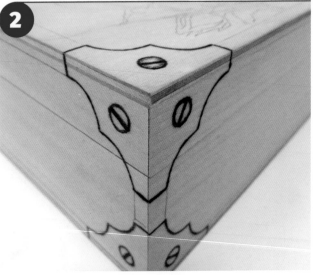

3 Next burn an even line along the edges of the box with a solid point such as the flow point, mini flow point, or ball stylus.

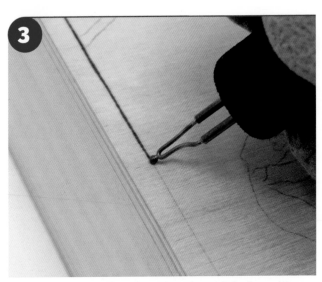

2 Continue burning the other brackets and screwheads on all sides of the box. (TIP: double-check that the corners line up correctly after transferring the pattern onto the box. Make minor adjustments if need be with a pencil before burning.)

SAFETY

Tip Some boxes are assembled with wood glue, which may be present on the edges. Be very careful when burning these areas and use an appropriate respirator to avoid breathing potentially toxic fumes. Also, these areas might produce a lot of carbon and gunk on the woodburning point, so extra cleaning may be needed.

Use a larger point to burn a solid black value on the edges of the box. Take your time and go over the area a few times to help achieve a deep black. (Remember the safety tip listed above.)

Use a small shading point or ball stylus to burn a gradient around the inner edge of each screwhead. This will give it a rounded appearance.

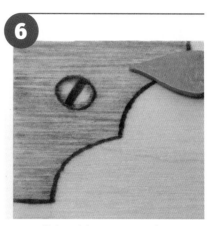

Burn a light mid-tone on each corner bracket. Try to make the area smooth and consistent in value.

After the edges and corner brackets are finished, use a smaller point and burn a smooth, even line around the lock and main elements of the design.

Use a small point to add shading to the lock on the front of the box.

9 Begin burning the leaves, twigs, and berries by burning the darker values with smooth strokes.

10 Burn the middle values and blend them into darker values.

11 Burn the lighter values of the branch.

12 Burn the darkest areas and values of the roses.

13 Burn the middle values and blend them into the darks.

Finish burning the roses by adding lighter mid-tones and blending them into the other areas.

Burn some shadows on the key by creating darker values on the undersides of the scrollwork and along the length of the key.

Blend those shadows with some mid-tones to give the key a more realistic appearance.

Once the elements are shaded, you can either add color or seal the wood.

Color Option!

I wanted this box to have an old-fashioned feeling about it, so I decided to not add color to the main design elements. However, I wanted the text to be more noticeable, so I added a bright red colored pencil to the larger text. If you don't want color, feel free to burn the text instead.

FOLLOW YOUR PASSION

This woodburning features a powerful message and simple elements, but the textured background puts emphasis on the smoother areas.

Materials
- Unfinished wood (approximately 8" x 10" [20 x 25cm])
- Pattern (see page 141)
- Graphite paper and red pen (to transfer the image)
- Fine-grit sandpaper (to sand graphite lines and fix errors)
- Woodburning unit
- Woodburning pens or points

Optional
- Colored pencils

Suggested Tips

Text and Outlines		Shading		Stippling	

1.5mm (¹⁄₁₆") Ball
Stylus (Razertip)
Heat Level: 5–7

Mini Flow Point
(Walnut Hollow
Versa-Tool)
Heat Level: Max

Medium Spoon
Shader (Razertip)
Heat Level: 5–10

Shading Point (Walnut
Hollow Versa-Tool)
*Heat Level:
Orange–Max*

3mm (¹⁄₈") Ball Stylus
(Razertip)
Heat Level: 5–7

Flow Point (Walnut
Hollow Versa-Tool)
Heat Level: Max

1

Begin by burning a dark outline around the outside of the text and each group of elements. This helps create a heat buffer for the next step.

2

Use a ball point or a flow tip and gently press it into the wood on the outer edges of the dark outline that you created in the previous step. Burn as close to the outline as possible without burning the subject. The medium-sized points won't fit in all of the tight spots but do the best you can, and then use a smaller point to burn the remaining areas.

Stippling can be quite time consuming and creates a lot of carbon build-up on the point. Take your time and keep the points clean or switch back and forth between two burners.

Continue burning the stippling around all the elements.

3

Continue pressing the point into the wood to fill in the negative space of the background with stippling. You can either keep the dots random or create a design if you'd like.

Finish the background with stippling.

Tip When burning the outer edges with stippling, it's easy for the point to accidentally slip off the side and burn the beveled area below. To avoid this, try to keep the burner vertical and press down slowly with minimal pressure.

But if you get accidental burns, use sandpaper to carefully remove the errors.

4 Begin burning all of the smooth leaves with a shading point. Burn a subtle line through each leaf and add more shading to the leaves that are behind others.

5 Start burning the bird with a shading point on higher heat. Focus on burning the darkest values, including the eye, wing outlines, and tail feathers.

6 Continue creating the bird by burning the middle values and blending them into the darks.

7 Finish the bird by turning the burner down to a lower temperature and slowly burning the lighter values. Be sure to blend these lighter areas with the mid-tones.

When burning the flowers, use a lower temperature and lightly outline the petals of each flower.

LIGHTS
MID-TONES
DARKS

The basics of rose petals: The darker values will be where each petal dives underneath its neighbor. Create a gradient from the inside of each petal to its outside, but add a slight bit of shading to the outer edge of each petal to create the illusion of a rounding rose petal.

Remember that objects often look darker when farther away, and objects look lighter when closer to the viewer.

Complete the rose by burning each petal with a gentle gradient as suggested in the previous step.

Burn the other flower with a lower temperature and a shading point. The center of the flower will be quite dark, but add soft shading on the outer edges of each petal.

12

Burn the rosehips and leaves with a shading point.

13

Finish the project by burning the remaining elements such as twigs, berries, and pine needles. Sign your woodburning. For this project, I simply burned my initials in the shadows of a leaf and signed my full name on the back side.

Color Option!

I absolutely love the vibrant colors in this project! I used Prismacolor® colored pencils and followed a theme of greens, yellows, and reds to evoke a feeling of approaching autumn.

Level 3 Project:

BON APPÉTIT WOODEN PLATE

Materials
- Unfinished wooden plate (approximately 11" x 11" [28 x 28cm])
- Pattern (see page 142)
- Graphite paper and red pen (to transfer the image)
- Fine-grit sandpaper (to sand graphite lines and fix errors)
- Woodburning unit
- Woodburning pens or points

Optional
- Acrylic paint or colored pencils
- Paintbrushes
- Clear coat

This is a unique project that features both positive and negative space. It builds on the basics of simple outlines and creates a sense of depth with shading.

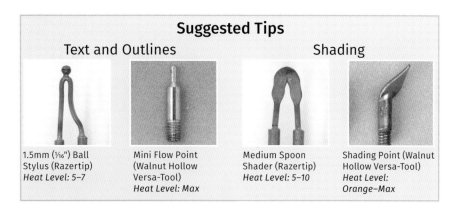

1

Begin by using graphite paper to transfer the pattern onto the wood. Next, use a small- to medium-sized point to burn an outline around the text and the negative spaces around the olive wreath of the outer edge of the plate. If you are comfortable and familiar with the woodburning pen, you can burn these outlines with long, smooth strokes. However, if you are still learning to use the tools, or have shaky hands, you might try burning the outlines with shorter, more controlled strokes.

Take your time to burn a solid, dark outline around each of the major elements in the project, except for the olive branch in the center of the plate.

Tip Remember to always place the point on the wood gradually, burn the line, and then lift the point off the wood smoothly. This helps avoid the dreaded stop spot.

Continue using a small- or medium-sized point to fill in the outlined areas with solid black or a pattern of your choice. (Feel free to be creative and use stippling, hatching, or crosshatching instead of solid black.) When burning a dark black, remember to work in a slow and even manner. Burning too quickly can produce a patchy, brown shade instead of a solid black. Outlining first will also help to avoid accidental overburn on your main subject.

Start on the outer border and burn the individual olives using a shading or universal point. Burn the darkest values first and be sure to leave the outer edges lighter so you can blend them with the lighter shades in the next step.

Use the same point to burn the lighter shades of the olives and softly blend the lighter shades into the darker ones for a more 3D effect. Repeat this on all the remaining olives, except for the ones in the center.

Tip Since the center olives are the focal point of the project, it helps to practice on the smaller olives around the border first. This develops your eye to see the subtle changes between shades and provides many practical "trial runs" before burning the olives in the center of the plate.

5

After burning the olives, use a shading point or ball tip on a medium/low setting to burn a light outline around each leaf, including the middle stem line. This step is optional, but it can really help you to see each individual leaf and create more definition later.

6

Lightly shade the leaves that appear closest to you or on top of the other leaves. (We will create depth and dimension to the olive wreath by keeping the topmost leaves lighter and burn them darker as they recede from view.)

7

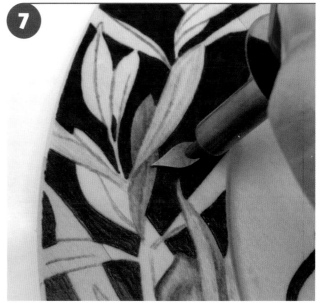

Shade the leaves underneath the top ones with a medium value.

Burn the leaves on the bottom with a darker mid-tone value. This will help create the illusion of depth by pushing the darker leaves away from the viewer's eye.

Now that you've had an opportunity to practice burning olives and leaves, it's time to create the focal point of the woodburning. Start by using a lower temperature to burn a light outline around the olives and leaves in the center of the piece.

Use a shading point to burn the darkest areas of the olives in the center of the burning. Remember to avoid burning a hard outline on the shaded areas. Keep things soft and a little blurry so you can blend them later.

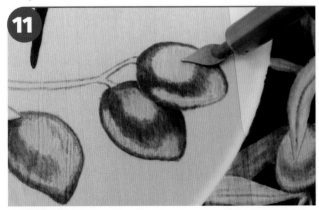

Use lower temperatures and softer shading to burn the lightest areas of the olives.

Blend the darker values with the lighter values to create a soft and rounded appearance to the olives.

13

Finish the woodburning by shading the leaves in the center of the project. The leaves that seem closest to the viewer will be lighter, and those that appear farther away will be darker. You can also burn a little more on the bottom side of each leaf to create the illusion of a light source up above.

COLOR OPTION!

If you'd like to add a splash of color to this woodburned plate, have fun with some acrylic paint! Your woodburned tones will be more visible if you apply extra water to the paint to create a semi-transparent wash. If you want paint that will be opaque, then use more solid paint and less water. Or you can use colored pencils instead.

NOTE: You can apply a clear coat over the woodburning and acrylic paint, but this wooden plate should be for decorative use only. Please do not eat on this plate.

GALLERY

I am constantly growing and changing as an artist, and this is a collection featuring some of my favorite woodburning projects I've created over the years. While this is a beginner's book, I'd like to encourage you all to start small but dream big! Once you learn the basics of pyrography, there's nothing that you can't create with practice and passion.

"MASSIVE"
11" X 19" (28 X 48CM) BASSWOOD ROUND
TOOL: WALNUT HOLLOW CREATIVE
VERSA-TOOL
REFERENCE PHOTO BY DIANA GRANT

While teaching myself how to woodburn, I started doing more research on the art and learned that basswood was one of the better types of wood to burn. I started experimenting more and more and created this woodburning of a bison we saw in Yellowstone National Park. It was a great learning experience for me because of the varied textures, and each one required a different technique to create. After I created this project, I joined Facebook and realized that there were multitudes of artists creating pyrography. It was incredibly inspirational, and I started sharing some of my artwork. Much to my surprise, many people wanted to know how I made this woodburning, and I was blown away at the support and encouragement of my fellow pyrographic artists.

This was a crucial turning point in my artistic path and turned me toward teaching others. I created my first instructional tutorial for this project and posted it on YouTube. Much to my surprise, the video was very well received, and artists began requesting more tips and information. This experience pushed me to create my first of many instructional DVDs, and then turned me to writing instructional books for the art of pyrography.

Sometimes we are asked to grow beyond our comfort zones. This takes courage and belief: the courage to try, and the belief that you can accomplish more than you know.

Autumn is my favorite season. I have spent most of my life in the beautiful mountains of Colorado, and I love taking walks during the fall and watching as the golden aspen leaves drift to the ground. During one such walk, I took a photo of a leaf nestled on the gravel road shortly after a rainstorm. At that time, I knew I had to create this woodburning. I fell in love with the wondrous textures of this piece, and the light source creates a full sense of depth. This was my first attempt at burning water droplets, and I later used this experience to create a step-by-step tutorial on my *Shading* DVD.

"GOLD ON THE ROCKS"
7" X 10" (18 X 25CM) BASSWOOD OVAL WITH LIVE EDGE
TOOL: WALNUT HOLLOW CREATIVE VERSA-TOOL
PRISMACOLOR COLORED PENCILS ADDED
REFERENCE PHOTO BY MINISA ROBINSON

"BIGHORN AT CLEMENTS MOUNTAIN"
8" X 10" (20 X 25CM) BASSWOOD PLAQUE
TOOL: WALNUT HOLLOW CREATIVE VERSA-TOOL
COLORED PENCILS AND ACRYLIC PAINT ADDED

I had been woodburning for a couple years and started dabbling with adding color to my pyrographic art pieces, but the piece above was a very experimental project from the beginning. When I planned this woodburning, I fully intended to paint over the burning with acrylic paint, which I had never tried before. So, I referenced one of my favorite oil paintings by my father (he is a professional landscape oil painting artist). This was a huge growth project to cross the boundaries of "pure" pyrography and combine my favorite aspects of realism and color.

Don't let the norms of society limit your potential! Sometimes the path not taken can lead you to a beautiful place.

"CHAOS"
16" X 26" (41 X 66CM) BASSWOOD
TOOL: WALNUT HOLLOW CREATIVE VERSA-TOOL
PRISMACOLOR COLORED PENCILS ADDED
REFERENCE PHOTO BY MATTHEW MALKIEWICZ

This is my all-time favorite woodburning that I've created to date. My husband has a strong love of trains, and I'm captivated by the energy and fury of the older locomotives. This type of project was on my "bucket list" for many years until I finally found the perfect blend of train and smoke (thanks, Matthew Malkiewicz). Mr. Malkiewicz is a phenomenal photographer who specializes in train photography, and he was kind enough to allow me permission to reference his photos for this piece. I digitally combined two different photos to create this composition and then got to work.

"Chaos" was created on a custom-cut 16" x 26" (41 x 66cm) piece of basswood and took me over 60 hours of burning. It was the biggest project that I had attempted at the time, and I worked on it little by little over the course of a year.

This project taught me the importance of perseverance and the joys of seeing a dream come to fruition through hard work and patience.

I strongly recommend creating artwork that stirs your soul. Find your passion and see it through to the end, regardless if you think you're "good enough" or not. One of the best ways to grow is to attempt projects that may be beyond your current level. The lessons learned are often more important than the task completed.

"MAROON BELLS"
20" X 16" (51 X 41CM) BASSWOOD
TOOL: WALNUT HOLLOW CREATIVE VERSA-TOOL
REFERENCE PHOTO FROM PIXABAY

"KINGFISHER"
11" X 14" (28 X 36CM) BASSWOOD PLAQUE
TOOL: WALNUT HOLLOW CREATIVE VERSA-TOOL
COLORED PENCILS ADDED
REFERENCE PHOTO BY GARY JONES

"STANDING GRIZZLY BEAR"
9" X 11" (23 X 28CM) BASSWOOD PLANK
TOOL: WALNUT HOLLOW CREATIVE VERSA-TOOL
PRISMACOLOR COLORED PENCILS ADDED
REFERENCE PHOTO BY DIANA GRANT

"THIRSTY TIGER"
8" X 10" (20 X 25CM) BASSWOOD PLAQUE
TOOL: WALNUT HOLLOW CREATIVE VERSA-TOOL
PRISMACOLOR COLORED PENCILS ADDED
REFERENCE PHOTO BY EMMANUEL KELLER

"A MOMENT OF REST"
12" X 16" (30 X 41CM) BASSWOOD PLANK
TOOL: WALNUT HOLLOW CREATIVE VERSA-TOOL
PRISMACOLOR COLORED PENCILS ADDED
REFERENCE PHOTO FROM PIXABAY

Minisa Robinson

"OWL ON A LOG"
8" X 10" (20 X 25CM) BASSWOOD PLAQUE
TOOL: WALNUT HOLLOW CREATIVE VERSA-TOOL
PRISMACOLOR COLORED PENCILS ADDED
REFERENCE PHOTO BY SUE DUDLEY

"MOTION"
11" X 14" (28 X 36CM) BASSWOOD PLAQUE
TOOL: WALNUT HOLLOW CREATIVE VERSA-TOOL
PRISMACOLOR COLORED PENCILS ADDED
REFERENCE PHOTO BY MICHELLE FAN: WILDLIFE
REFERENCE PHOTOS

"DIANA"
SMALL TISSUE BOX
TOOL: WALNUT HOLLOW CREATIVE VERSA-TOOL
PRISMACOLOR COLORED PENCILS ADDED
REFERENCE PHOTOS BY DIANA GRANT

"MAMA BEAR"
8.5" X 26" (22 X 66CM) BUTTERNUT
TOOL: WALNUT HOLLOW CREATIVE VERSA-TOOL
ACRYLIC PAINT AND COLORED PENCILS ADDED
REFERENCE PHOTO BY LORRAINE LOGAN

Temperature Chart (p. 28)
Photocopy at 200%

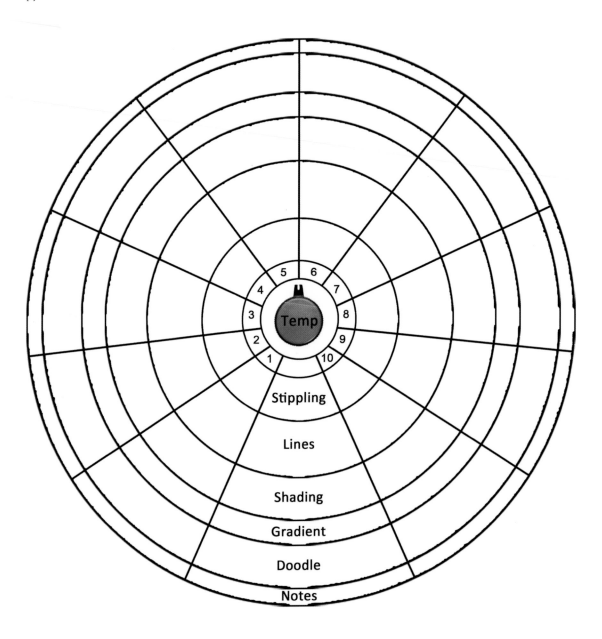

Bookmark (p. 56)

Photocopy at 100%

Mountain Bangle Bracelet (p. 60)

Photocopy at 125%

Fun and Foxy Keychain (p. 67)

Photocopy at 100%

Feather Pendants (p. 85)

Photocopy at 100%

Snowflake Coasters (p. 64)

Photocopy at 200%

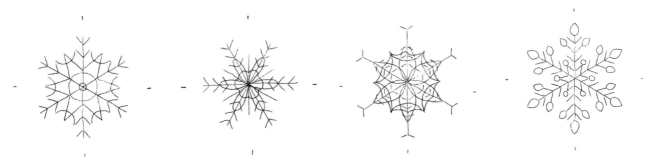

Toilet Paper Roll (p. 30)

Photocopy at 200%

Country Jar (p. 96)
Photocopy at 167%

Coffee Time (p. 69)

Photocopy at 100%

WOODBURNING PROJECTS AND PATTERNS FOR BEGINNERS

Welcome Sign (p. 58)

Photocopy at 200%

Wolf Gradient (p. 72)

Photocopy at 125%

Mandala (p. 75)

Photocopy at 167%

Adventure Key Holder (p. 78)

Photocopy at 125%

Always Bee Kind (p. 81)

Photocopy at 125%

Serving Tray (p. 88)

Photocopy at 167%

Memory Box (p. 101)
Photocopy at 125%

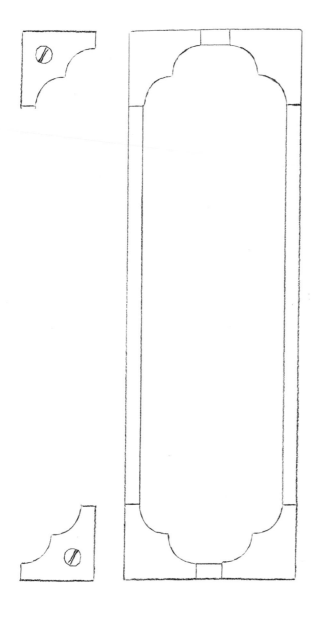

Family Frame (p. 92)

Photocopy at 125%

Follow Your Passion (p. 106)

Photocopy at 125%

Bon Appétit Wooden Plate (p. 112)

Photocopy at 167%

INDEX

ABOUT THE AUTHOR

Minisa Robinson was raised in the mountains and backcountry of Colorado and grew up with a strong appreciation of art. She is the daughter of a professional artist, her father, and was blessed to watch him capture the world around him using oil paints. Minisa is self-taught in many areas of art, including oil painting, sketching, graphic arts, acrylic painting, and alcohol inks. However, she is most known for her realistic woodburnings, also known as pyrographic art.

Minisa stumbled across pyrography by accident in 2009 when exploring the art of woodcarving. Since then, she has taught herself to create highly detailed woodburnings and has also become a leader and teacher in her field. She pushes the limits of pyrography and encourages others to view the art in a new light. Minisa enjoys a challenge and continually explores new techniques and ideas while growing as an artist.

After graduating high school, Minisa spent 12 years as a self-taught graphic designer and published state-level newspapers, in addition to co-creating an online e-magazine. She now spends most of her time as a homeschooling, work-at-home mother of three. "It can be crazy sometimes!" she said. "It's never easy juggling the responsibilities of being a parent, teacher, homemaker, or artist, but it's especially challenging to do each one every day." Challenges aside, Minisa wouldn't have it any other way. "My family is my everything. I absolutely love being with them each day and watching them learn and grow."